The Believable
Corporation

Other books by Roger M. D'Aprix

IN SEARCH OF A CORPORATE SOUL

STRUGGLE FOR IDENTITY: THE SILENT REVOLUTION AGAINST CORPORATE CONFORMITY

HOW'S THAT AGAIN? A GUIDE TO EFFECTIVE WRITTEN AND ORAL COMMUNICATION IN BUSINESS

The Believable Corporation

ROGER M. D'APRIX

A Division of
American Management Associations

Library of Congress Cataloging in Publication Data

D'Aprix, Roger M
  The believable corporation.

    Bibliography: p.
    Includes index.
    1. Communication in personnel management. 2. Com-
munication in management. I. Title.
HF5549.5.C6D34   658.4'5   77–22360

© *1977 AMACOM*
A division of American Management Associations, New York.
All rights reserved. Printed in the United States of America.

Second Printing,

For Theresa
in thanksgiving for your love,
your companionship, your generosity,
and your free spirit.

Acknowledgments

THIS has been a difficult book to write since it represents almost 20 years of personal experience as a professional communicator in a large organization. What I should really acknowledge is the opportunity I have been given over the years by a number of such organizations to study them from the perspective of an employee and a working professional. I do acknowledge that opportunity and the willingness of the likes of General Electric, Bell and Howell, and Xerox to permit me to learn what I think I know.

My longest tenure has been with Xerox, a company that is deservedly recognized as one of the most enlightened in the world. Xerox continues to be the source of my own belief in the possibility of responsible corporate behavior.

Having said that, let me state for the record that none of the ideas I express in this book should be construed to have the endorsement or approval of Xerox. This book is a personal statement of my peculiar view of organizational communication.

I should also acknowledge my many colleagues in the employee communications business, who have been patient enough to listen to my ideas and to set me straight through the years. That list is far too long to itemize, but they certainly know who they are. Ours is an emerging specialty that reflects the rapid changes that are occurring in corporate life. I hope that my thoughts serve to clarify some of what is happening in this specialty and to open further dialog.

Finally, I should like to point out that all the hypothetical "case histories" I cite in this book are products of my imagination. Any resemblances to real American companies—living or dead—is sheer coincidence.

Thanks to careful record-keeping, I now know for the sake of those who are interested in such things that it takes me about 200 hours to write a book like this one. The trouble is that those hours are spent at my kitchen table after a full day's work. They are also spent, I might add, at the expense of my family who would otherwise be able to communicate with me, use me as a handy man (that's an inside joke), or lay claim to my services in some fashion.

To all those who suffered my glazed stare and general inattention as I made still another run at fame and glory, I offer my gratitude. Thank you for understanding. To Tom Gannon and the staff at AMACOM I offer my gratitude for outstanding professional support.

Roger M. D'Aprix

Contents

. . . Do not say things. What you are stands over you the while, and thunders so that I cannot hear what you say to the contrary.

RALPH WALDO EMERSON

Introduction

WHEN I first began writing this book, I wanted to explore what the changing values and aspirations of the employee workforce have done to the never-easy problem of employee communication. But the more I thought about that problem, the more it led me back to the general problem of institutional credibility and its causes.

I learned perhaps for the nine hundred and ninety-ninth time in my career as a communications professional that you cannot examine the problem of human communication in isolation. To do so means to disregard the context and the environment that affect it so profoundly. And we end up looking at a different problem from the one we began with. Instead of examining the *nature* of such communication and why and how it takes place, we begin to examine the *techniques* of communication, as though their mastery were the real answer to our problems.

And so we blithely ignore human psychology, philosophy, history, and the values that underlie people's communication behavior and concentrate on finding ways to perfect the media and the programs that will finally "get our message across" to "them." I've lost count of the times I've heard an ardent speaker tell a roomful of fascinated listeners how to *get the message across*. . . .

This approach to communication and to credibility reminds me of a fascination my five-year-old son Tony has for the small starfish that nestle in the shallow water in the rocks and crevices in front of the cottage in Maine where we vacation. He gets impatient with peering at them in the water and trying to understand their behavior, so he searches for a stick and gently slides one of them up out of the cold ocean water onto a nearby rock where he can get a better look. He is always disappointed as the starfish struggles to swim off the dry rock and back into the cold, life-giving ocean. Plucked from the ocean, the starfish reveals much less of its real essence than it does in the weeds of the shallow pools left behind by the tide. And if it's kept out of the water long enough, it dries up and dies in a lifeless form that resembles a starfish but isn't.

Unfortunately, too much of our knowledge about human communication and about the techniques for improving it are based on this kind of analysis where, in effect, we lay it on a rock until it stops squirming and then study its rigid corpse. I have tried very hard in this book not to study communication corpses. So much for what the book does not do.

I suppose that among people who have studied the nature of organizational communication, and especially the credibility of corporations, I am something of a radical. I believe that the communication process in and of itself is essential to our humanity and that it is good. In my judgment it is not merely a means to attaining a number of worthy organizational goals. I accept it as a worthwhile end in itself.

This assertion will disconcert a good many people in business who see organizational communication only as a tool for giving people information that will make them more efficient in achieving the objectives of the organization. I think that this rationale, besides being shortsighted, is the reason that so many people in organizations regard communication impatiently as a process that breaks down far too often and takes too much valuable time away from "getting the work done."

My view is radically different. I believe that adults employed by any organization should be treated as adults and that their personal stake in that organization—no matter how small or large that stake may seem—should be respected. In short, they deserve to be communicated with and to be recognized as *members* of the organization. I think that intellectually, most people would agree with that assumption and maybe even applaud it.

The trouble is that our behavior in organizations is almost exactly the opposite. We tend to act as though people were just another organizational resource. In effect, we say, "If you don't like it here, why don't you quit and go somewhere else?" Or we play that most malicious game of pretending to care about people and their contributions and then manipulating them for the sake of the organization, without regard for *their* welfare, *their* needs, or *their* desires. We grind them down here. We dehumanize them there. We show them who the boss is at each turn. Sometimes we do it brutally and openly, sometimes subtly and almost imperceptibly.

But whatever form these actions take, they are based on the assumption that people really don't count for very much, that there are other priorities that are so compelling, so threatening, or so enticing that people can and should only be used. The other priorities normally are held high in the air as banners for us to rally under—things like production quotas, earnings growth, shareholder dividends, and lots of other organizational targets that can be quantified and analyzed and agonized over. These things are so real and so important to the very survival of the business that they often can become the ends that justify some rather shabby human means.

Perhaps that's why we in organizations spend so much time talking about the need for better communication. We feel guilty about our lack of attention to human needs, so we talk almost compulsively about how communication is our No. 1 problem, our No. 1 organizational need—like the drunk who is forever swearing he's going on the wagon . . . tomorrow, or the day after tomorrow. And he goes on drinking. In organizations we keep saying we've got to communicate better. And then we go on ignoring the whole issue in our headlong rush to attain other priorities and other goals.

A surprising number of people see nothing wrong or illogical in any of this. They often follow out a conventional wisdom about people management that says you can either be hard on people or soft on people. If you're tough, they'll respect you and produce. If you're soft, they'll take advantage of you and be unproductive. The dichotomy is nice and neat, but like most dichotomies, it's grossly oversimplified and inaccurate.

Perhaps the greatest need that humans bring to their work is their need to understand its meaning and their role in the scheme of things. In American society in particular, we are our work. Literally, we *are* mechanics, lawyers, bus drivers, lathe operators, school teachers, or whatever. For better or worse, our identity and our status derive from these roles we play out for one another.

Given this fact, it is not hard to understand why the need for information on the job and the need for human communication are so intense. The desire for job information and for human reaction and interaction is not a casual matter. These items are not luxuries. They are the gut-level needs.

Some fascinating work done a few years ago at Texas Instruments demonstrated that people essentially have four kinds of job needs that follow a predictable pattern. In the beginning, they have a consuming need for job mastery. It is essential for them to learn the ropes of the new job so that they can be reasonably proficient.

Once they have mastered the job, they need to know the ground rules of the organization. If you do such and such, what will be the likely consequences? Or, conversely, if you don't do such and such, what will happen? In a word, they desire "predictability." Once that's satisfied, they move to their third-level need, which is much more complex. They want some sort of evidence, no matter how skimpy or tentative, that they are appreciated, that they are members in good standing of the organization, and that they are, in fact, loved. Only when they attain this level of satisfaction on the job—if they ever do—are they ready to give their allegiance. At that point they are ready to give of their talents and their energy with little or no reservation.*

The road to the satisfaction of these needs is not smooth, and for some people—perhaps for most of us—it leads straight to a dead end.

Those who see the organizational experience only as the disciplining and directing of people so that they can perform their work in a productive and orderly fashion will probably never understand the subtleties and the agonies of organizational communication. Their view is that open and free-flowing communication is a burden, a time waster, an unnecessary expenditure of their energy and imagination.

* Earl R. Gomersall, in an address to the Rochester Chapter of the American Institute of Industrial Engineers, Rochester, New York, November 6, 1969.

Today, however, with changing aspirations and values as well as the changing nature of work from mostly manual labor to mostly service or knowledge labor, it is hard to see how anyone can retain this reactionary view. The one real given of this book is that organizations have an obligation to communicate honestly and openly with the public at large and especially with their own people.

Let's see how corporations might do the job more effectively and more believably than they have in the past.

CHAPTER I

The Employee Audience: Problems and Issues

SOME amazing things are happening in the area of organizational communication. They are exciting, and they are important. But they have largely gone unnoticed.

When I took my first communications job in 1959, I was hired into a corporate world that was autocratic, not to say tyrannical. Its leaders were powerful men who did not hesitate to use their power in subtle and not so subtle ways to control the behavior of the people who were part of their organizations. One held his or her job by virtue of doing what those in power wanted done when they wanted it done. The system was regarded as good, and woe be unto anyone who decided to test or challenge it.

I remember one corporate martinet whose marketing manager (a man considerably brighter and more capable than his boss) disagreed in public about a new policy the boss was advocating. The occasion was a meeting of the senior managers of the division. The marketing manager made his brief argument and sat down. Since no one had ever dared challenge the boss publicly, there was an almost audible gasp. When the meeting was over, the boss summoned his errant manager and fired him on the spot. He had committed the unpardonable sin.

I don't think there are too many companies where that scenario would be repeated today. Certainly there are arbitrary firings, but good people are not thrown on the scrap heap merely because they have the nerve to disagree.

There are probably two major reasons for this change. One has been the erosion of a whole host of "givens" about work and a person's relationship to the organization that employs him or her. The other is the increasing sophistication and educational backgrounds of employees as we shift from mainly manual, blue-collar work to mainly knowledge, white-collar work.

In the old days, the employee audience was conditioned to believe and to accept on faith the premise that the boss was the boss and that he knew best. Perhaps that attitude is best typified by the work-simplification pioneer Frederick Winslow Taylor, who used to say that a worker had to know only two things on the job: One, who is my boss? And, two, what does he want me to do right at this moment? In fairness to Taylor, he was talking about a very different kind of work environment than most of us know today, but his attitude certainly was the accepted one. And it is not difficult to find people today who would still agree with that uncomplicated formula.

On the whole, however, today's audience is more conditioned to question and to disbelieve. For example, a decade ago pollster Lou Harris reported that 55 percent of the American public had "high confidence" in business. By 1975, that figure had fallen to only 18 percent. Business organizations, like a good many other of our institutions, are perceived as taking care of their own parochial interests and of the interests of the powerful people who lead them. That perception, whether it is factual or not, has made it very difficult for institutions to formulate and deliver credible messages to both internal and external audiences.

To a significant extent institutions are victims of what Daniel Yankelovich indelicately calls "the Bullshit syndrome." As the name implies, the audience's mental set is one of extreme distrust and cynicism about what's coming. It could be argued that a large portion of this distrust is richly deserved, especially with the recent revelations of such things as corporate bribes and kickbacks.

But the vast majority of corporate officials and executives are truthful and honorable. In my own experience that assertion would cover about 95 percent of the people I've had close dealings with as a communicator. They may slant the message somewhat to reflect their own bias, but that is no more than any of us do in practically all our communication with the rest of the world.

If, like the rest of the American public, the employee audience is more skeptical of the message, and I know from my twenty years of work experience in three separate corporations that it is, what have managers and communications people done to combat this skepticism or at least to make allowances for it? Incredibly, the answer is, Not much.

For example, on the employee communication side of the house, it is still not unusual for a bright young female secretary who is underemployed to be tapped to be the next "house organ" editor. Although the employee audience is obviously one of the most important that any business organization must address itself to, it is often one of the most neglected. Let me unfold a short and sad hypothetical tale of what happens in all too many American business organizations.

Gretchen Greensleeves is hired by National Bank straight out of the State College for Teachers, where she minored in English composition. She's no great shakes as a typist, but the bank's senior vice president, who can't spell or punctuate, thinks she's a whiz at correcting his correspondence. One day an Equal Employment Opportunity representative shows up at the bank to inquire about the bank's affirmative action program and its hiring and promotion practices for women. One of the cases the representative takes considerable interest in is Gretchen's. How come a four-year college graduate is employed as a glorified typist?

At about the same time, the man who has produced the bank's employee magazine for the last 25 years retires. The senior vice president remembers that Gretchen can spell and is "just outstanding" with commas and semicolons. Suddenly she is the new editor of the bank's primary communications tool, *The National Banker.*

In response to her plea for help, he simply tells her to "do it the same way old Ed did." And that's exactly what she does after she goes through the file cabinet of old issues. The results are predictable and lead most of her readers to the feeling that Robert Townsend once described as "like going down in warm maple syrup for the third time."

Gretchen continues to put out a folksy magazine that she writes laboriously for, takes the pictures for, and lays out with the help of her patient printer. It goes to 3,000 National Bank employees in six counties and contains: A Message from the President, pictures of retirees, a list of long-service awards, a welcome to the new employees, a know-your-benefits column, boring articles on such things as how the Federal Reserve System is organized and other pieces she can plagiarize from various banking publications, a list of birthdays, engagements, births, and death notices, a descriptive piece on one of the bank's major departments and how it functions, and finally the classified ads of employee property for sale or trade.

Unfortunately, while Gretchen fiddles, National Bank is on fire. The tellers are organizing a union, the officers are a tight little clique who share no information with their subordinates, the secretaries are overworked and largely ignored, and turnover is the highest in the area. Still National points with pride to *The National Banker* as evidence of its sterling efforts to communicate with employees. The payoff comes when Gretchen submits her publication to a local editors' group and wins a gold medal, mostly because her printer is able each month to convert her copy, her amateurish photos, and the endless lists of names of people "to be recognized" into a decent-looking publication. Never mind that National Bank people read only the want ads and dismiss the rest as sophomoric. Management believes that Gretchen is doing a great job in making people feel a part of the National Bank "family."

The inevitable question must be asked. Why is National Bank management naive enough to believe that this sort of communication works? The answer is that no one ever takes the time to find out if it is or isn't working. And make no mistake about it: National Bank is a hypothetical case, but there are thousands of "Nationals" throughout the country. Nor is this problem confined to the small organization with very limited resources. It is a problem for a good many large and prestigious organizations that treat the employee communication problem just about as casually.

In general, the problem either reflects a total lack of understanding of employee motivation and employee attitudes and values, or reflects indifference. The management that cares about such things rarely allows this situation to go uncorrected. It is true that often there are other priorities in a business that make the employee communication issue seem to be less important, but this is obviously a shortsighted position when the success of the organization can be profoundly affected by the quality of communication with employees. And here, of course, I am not limiting the issue merely to an employee publication. I mean the whole gamut of techniques that we use to be certain that employees are being communicated with effectively.

Let's go back to National Bank for a minute. What are the results of its cavalier approach to employee communication? The overall result is a terrible credibility problem. If an organization has substantial employee problems, such as those National has, with its tight-lipped officers and overworked secretaries, and if it is publishing a glossy magazine that never acknowledges that there is a single problem in the organization and that talks about the National "family," it is clear that people will begin to ask questions.

They will question the sanity and the intelligence of the people who publish such stuff, and they will certainly compare their everyday experience with the picture presented in the magazine. When these two things are inconsistent with one another, people will be both confused and angry. And they will certainly long for someone to tell them the truth. More will be said about this subject in the next chapter.

First, let us examine briefly what is happening to the attitudes and values of people at our hypothetical bank—and in every real business organization in the country. Much has been written about this subject, so I will not try to develop it in detail. But it is important that we remind ourselves that today's employee audience has different expectations, values, and beliefs than the employee audience of as little as ten years ago. The failure to recognize this change leaves management in the absurd position of speaking to its employees in what is essentially a foreign language. In far too many organizations the leadership states its hopes, goals, and priorities for the organization in terms that mean little or nothing to those who must accomplish them. And then that same leadership is perplexed by the lack of employee commitment to the organization and the lack of understanding of its problems.

The trouble is that the two groups do not have a common perspective. Or they simply disagree about what needs to be done and why it needs to be done. More often than not, this disagreement is implicit rather than explicit, for how can two parties really be said to disagree when they don't comprehend each other's positions? And this often is the case at least between management and its knowledge workers—the people who contribute not their physical labor but their expert knowledge to the success of the business. Ironically, skilled and unskilled laborers often have a clearer perception of how they fit into the scheme of things by virtue of their being represented by a bargaining unit and by having more tangible job responsibilities. The fact of their representation usually forces a communication relationship during bargaining as well as during the normal course of registering contract grievances.

The knowledge worker, on the other hand, is left almost exclusively to his or her perceptions of what management is up to and why. Clearly, this is a dangerous game for management to play. As Peter Drucker has pointed out, top-down communication alone does not work because it is the employee's perceptions that determine the outcome of the communication process. The management that concludes that it need not explain itself and can leave its employee audience to draw its own conclusions is playing with fire. This is essentially what the National Banks of the world are doing by not talking about the issues.

Let's see how dangerous that game can be by looking at the perceptual problem for a moment. Drucker and others correctly point out that communication "downward" does not work. The primary reason for its failure is that it focuses on what "we" want to say rather than on what the audience needs and wants to know. By definition, it ignores the fact that communication is the act of the recipient, that it is his or her *perceptions* that control the outcome of the process. If we continually focus on the message that we want to communicate, without regard for how that message is being perceived by the recipients, we can unintentionally create one hell of a problem for everyone.

Drucker makes the point that downward communication can work only *after* it has been informed and shaped by *upward* communication. In other words, downward communication is a *response* to the values, beliefs, and aspirations of those who are receiving the message. And if management ignores or does not understand those values, beliefs, and aspirations, downward communication will not work. It simply will not connect with its audience in the way that it must connect if there are to be *shared* perceptions of reality.[1]

Two lessons can be drawn. One, the successful communicator will always be probing the audience's values and beliefs *before* he or she attempts to develop a message that will connect. And, two, any management that does not have its ear to the ground cannot hope to communicate with its people.

There is also a third lesson that underscores the dual nature of organizational communication. Somehow the entire management group must be involved in continuous exchanges with its people on the really important issues. As Drucker puts it,

> There can be no communication if it is conceived as going from the "I" to the "Thou." Communication works only from one member of "us" to another. Communication in organization—and this may be the true lesson of our communication failure and the true measure of our communication need—is not a *means* of organization. It is the *mode* of organization.[2]

Clearly, neither National Bank nor any other organization can rely on the Gretchen Greensleeves of the world to carry the load. Even if they do their jobs well, this will not begin to solve the employee communication problem. The burden must be borne by every single manager in the organization, who must maintain relationships with his or her people that permit open and honest two-way communication on every issue of importance to the audience.

When this happens, the thoroughly professional communicator can *backstop* the manager's communication efforts with timely and informed formal communications that address the audience's real needs and concerns and that paint the same big picture for everyone in the organization.

If this does not happen to a significant degree in any given organization, then Ms. Greensleeves will be performing a cosmetic service that manages only to lull senior management into the belief that it is addressing the problem. If you are indifferent to results, the mere existence of company publications will at least give the *appearance* of communication.

Effective employee communication is a *total* proposition. It is good solid management communication at every single level of the organization, with the emphasis on two-way communication between the manager and the people he or she manages. And it is also a total program of formal communications that are consistent with audience needs and concerns and that are timely and complete. Any management that does not understand this point is not going to be able to deal effectively with the problem of intraorganizational communication.

Having said all this, let's examine the particular employee attitudes and values that compound the already difficult problem of organizational communication. Pretend for a moment that you are chief operating officer of XYZ Associates, a relatively new company that has been very successful in the computer business. Over the ten-year history of your firm, you have attracted large numbers of young, ambitious men and women who expect to contribute, to be well compensated, and to advance in their careers rather rapidly.

You perceive that there are perplexing problems in communicating with your employee audience. The basis of your concern is that there is an underlying layer of cynicism and disbelief in your audience. You are especially distressed because you have made a strong personal effort to be as open and as forthright as you possibly could in all your dealings with your people. But as the number of people at the company has grown, the mistrust and the cynicism have increased substantially.

Finally, you decide to call in an independent consultant to do some attitude surveying and to size up the audience. In his summary of XYZ's employee communication problems, your consultant reports that because of XYZ's emphasis on achieving very ambitious goals XYZ people have come to believe that they are operating in a rather hostile environment where political skill counts more than ability and where the emphasis is on short-term results rather than on the long-term good of the business. By and large, they feel used, and they believe that if the day ever comes when they have outlived their usefulness to XYZ, they will be shelved or dismissed.

With that perception they, predictably, feel very little personal loyalty to XYZ. They report that their work is often done in rather frenzied fashion and that they feel great concern about achieving anything less than outstanding results. Overlying all of this is an emerging concern that only women and minorities will advance in the coming months and years at XYZ. Young, white males are particularly apprehensive in this regard. And the minority group members as well as the women of XYZ are impatient about their situation and believe that not enough is being done to advance their interests.

When your consultant probes some of these perceptions, he finds that XYZ people believe that "the system" at XYZ gets in the way of results. They are irritated by what they feel is a growing bureaucracy in the company, and more and more their loyalty is to their own careers, rather than to XYZ. They are also particularly vocal about their desire for fulfillment on the job, claiming that they value this more than money or status. There is a good deal of discussion about the quality of life and what they owe themselves as people.

Another common concern is their desire to participate in the management process. They want to share in both information and decision making. Their perception is that XYZ management cares about their attitudes and is willing to make concessions to improve their morale. This seems to contradict their concern about "being used," but it is apparently a common view among XYZ people.

Finally, the consultant reports that most of the XYZ people surveyed did not feel that they were being properly trained, supervised, and evaluated by their bosses. They also felt that too much information was withheld from them by their bosses, although senior management was seen as willing to be candid.

The consultant concludes in his report to you that

your employee audience is indeed skeptical and that it has high expectations about work and about what the company owes the individual. At the same time, there is a good deal of apprehension about personal failure and one's ability to keep up in such a highly charged, competitive atmosphere.

This report presents some interesting questions for you as chief operating officer. For openers, how do you deal with the frank skepticism of your people about the company? How can you win the trust of the people you are trying to manage? This is no small question because you simply cannot communicate with someone who does not trust you.

A corporate bureaucracy is clearly spilling over the top of the corporate jar labeled XYZ. How do you cap it? How do you reassure everyone of equitable treatment and opportunity, particularly when short-term affirmative action requirements have to be met to satisfy the U.S. Equal Employment Opportunity laws? How do you persuade first-line and middle managers to function as managers and not merely as keepers of order? How do you get them to develop people for greater responsibility in the future? And on and on as you untangle the complex attitudes that are presented as part of the XYZ environment.

XYZ is just a hypothetical example, obviously, but it's not too far from the mark in defining some of the perplexing issues that face corporate leaders who are trying to deal with changing expectations and still meet the intense demands for business results. Only when you begin to examine these kinds of questions seriously are you looking at the full scope of the employee communication problem.

Some may object that what has been outlined here is the total problem of managing a business. That is absolutely correct because there is no way to manage a business effectively today without effective employee communication. The two processes go hand in hand. Employee communication that addresses itself to such traditional concerns as announcing service anniversaries, publishing pictures of retirees, and covering the Christmas party three months after the fact is about as connected to corporate reality as factory whistles, company stores, free Thanksgiving turkeys, and similar relics of the past.

Let's now remove you from the position of chief operating officer of XYZ and put you in charge of another hypothetical organization of a more traditional sort. Acme Chemical Company employs 20,000 people in one large facility. It is almost totally centralized both geographically and philosophically. You, together with your senior staff, pass on every single major decision or program that will be implemented at Acme. The company was founded in the 1890s and for years has dominated its marketplace.

Typically, your employees have come to you straight from high school, and in recent years from college, and have stayed with you for practically their full working careers. In general, there is an attitude among them that they are fortunate to be employed by Acme. The pay is good, the benefits are good, there is not very much pressure for the average worker, and even in management, the pace is not very taxing. Your people are often like well-fed tomcats, preening themselves in the sun of corporate success.

23

In this environment it is rare to hear a complaint. And rarely, if ever, does anyone knock the company, at least publicly. And if anyone does, there is sure to be an old-timer within earshot to remind the critic that "things could be a hell of a lot worse," that he remembers "the Depression when. . . ." And so the gripe is nipped before anyone has to look very hard at it and run the risk of admitting that he is not, after all, in the best of all possible worlds.

There is a sharp distinction at Acme between the professional people and the production workers. The two worlds are totally separate. There is an even sharper distinction between manager and subordinate. In general, line managers see themselves as the people who should control costs, closely supervise their people's workload and time, and meet schedules.

In general, despite the regimentation, there is an interesting paternalistic atmosphere in Acme. Pay and benefits are good, and layoffs are almost unheard of. A couple of years ago, a business school professor did some research at Acme on the value systems of Acme people. What he found tended to reinforce this view of a rather paternalistic organization in which people were contentedly slotted, largely according to their "time in grade."

When the professor broke his study down according to the positions of the people being surveyed, he found similar but slightly different aspirations at work. The production people seemed to want routine work that they could accomplish at a moderate work pace. They were very anxious to work with friendly people who were willing to break the monotony with some horseplay and "who could take a joke." And they were almost universal in their desire to have "a good boss who tells you what he wants you to do."

The clerical people at Acme were less interested in on-the-job pranks and kidding, but they did seem to have strong needs for job security and for rules that told them exactly what they were and were not supposed to do on the job. Two other values that ranked high on their list were loyalty and conformity. The secretaries, for example, were especially critical of what they perceived as lax standards of dress for their co-workers, particularly some of the younger women "who were even going bra-less in a business office."

Among professional and managerial people, the values were slightly different, but the same desires for a friendly and structured work environment were evident. Two strong desires expressed by this group were for harmony and for friendly work relationships. One high-level research manager reported with evident pleasure that he had been playing poker with the same group of co-workers every Friday night for 35 years.

The average young person who joins Acme can expect to move rather slowly through the Acme system, with its longish developmental cycles and new job assignments only every seven to eight years. It is not uncommon for someone to retire in a job only a notch or two higher than the one he began in. It is true that Acme has its "fast-track" performers, but they are generally regarded as "pushy" and "political." And the system has a way of taking some of the starch out of them in subtle and not so subtle ways.

The employee communication program at Acme

reflects much of the paternalism and the "you're-lucky-to-be-one-of-us" attitude that pervades the company. The "program" is a weekly eight-page newspaper that features some topic of company interest on the front page and then fills the next seven pages with stories about employee activities, picnics, employee hobbies off the job, pictures of retirees, and a full page of classified ads. Anyone who wanted any serious or informative material about Acme could not find it in this publication. He'd be better advised to read the business page of his local newspaper for such things. Though, in all honesty, he'd have his problems there too, because Acme public relations plays everything but new-product news extremely close to the vest. Local business editors normally expect "no comment" replies to almost any inquiry they make at Acme.

This tranquil picture is shaken for you as chief executive of Acme when you hire a consultant to conduct a full-blown employee attitude survey. Most of the attitudes are positive, but your consultant turns up some distressing findings behind the calm façade. Most of the negative findings have to do with the way Acme people are being managed by their immediate supervisors. The litany of the reactions goes about as follows:

- Employees have to carefully pick the time they talk to their supervisors.
- Supervisors tend to assume that their ideas are best. They rarely talk about company objectives or how the work group should address them.

- They give people about as much information as they think they need.
- Their performance expectations seem to change daily.
- They try to discourage their people from taking risks or changing traditional ways of doing things.
- When something goes wrong, they try mainly to find out whose fault it was.
- They rarely praise performance; they expect you to do an adequate job.

As chief executive, what do you do now? Can you or should you try to change a social system that seems to be dulling your people's creativity and initiative? What can you do about managers who don't communicate much of anything to their people except criticism and who actually discourage initiative and taking risks? Can your business tolerate building and perpetuating more corporate bureaucracy? After so many years in this system, can you modify the behavior of the old-timers? What will happen to your organization if competition should suddenly get stronger and force your company to be innovative and to step up the pace of the business? And, finally, will the changes in values occurring outside your corporate walls begin to filter in and shake some of the entrenched attitudes that discourage wave-making or aggressive pursuit of one's own career objectives or one's desire for a fulfilling job?

Obviously Acme and XYZ are practically at opposite ends of a continuum. But they do represent the kinds of practical problems that managements now face with their employee communication responsibilities. Because of the organization's age and because of the age of its employee base, not to mention the sort of business it is in, XYZ is a more contemporary organization that is likely to reflect more contemporary attitudes.

For the same reasons, Acme is a rather reactionary organization more attuned to the concerns and styles of earlier years. We are tempted to characterize such organizations as "good" or "bad" or as "progressive" or "regressive," but such labels can be misleading. Each organization in its own way provides a culture and an environment that is matched to the particular problems it is up against. The appropriateness of its principles and actions probably should be judged in relation to its problems rather than in strict value terms.

On the other hand, if you are a *member* of such an organization, living in its particular culture, its match with your own values and aspirations can become crucial. You spend a lot of your time and emotional energy in that culture. For the sake of your mental health and your personal goals, the fit must be a reasonable one. When it is possible for them to do so, people express the degree of fit by "voting with their feet" until they find a place that is, at its best, motivating and stimulating and, at its worst, tolerable.

One useful dichotomy for sorting out organizations, though it certainly smacks of a value judgment, is the one that characterizes them as "traditional" or "contemporary" or, in one case anyway, as "19th century" and "21st century." Traditional organizations like Acme are characterized as being more concerned with form and order. Typically, they are hierarchical in their organization, with most of the power concentrated at the top. They tend to be run rather autocratically, and much is made of seniority as the path to power.

When the major problem to be dealt with is maintaining order and preserving continuity, this is not a bad way to go. It is obvious, however, that such organizations can have so much structure that eventually they suffer a kind of corporate hardening of the arteries. When this happens in both humans and in organizations, it is likely that the capacity for rational thought and behavior will become impaired. The outcome for humans is early senility. The outcome for organizations is more likely to be mindless bureaucracy.

Certainly a society that experiences a good deal of change would do well to keep its organizations flexible enough to cope with that change. Otherwise they simply become anachronisms.

The question of organization is important in a variety of ways to the whole issue of communication. For example, in the highly traditional organization, communication is ritualized. Because so much depends on authority and power, it is essential to communicate in a style that makes the authority look rational, benevolent, and well informed. Otherwise people begin to challenge it. It is also important that people know and respect one another's office. Hence, there is considerable emphasis on communication up and down a chain of command. The worker is not permitted to air his grievances to his boss's boss without first seeking permission and approval. The motive is to maintain orderly lines of authority, but the practical result is to stifle dissent of any kind.

Similarly, communication from the top of the organization is supposed to be passed down the chain of command from management level to management level. There are two familiar problems with that approach to top-down communication. One is that the message gets filtered and refiltered at every level, and it is badly distorted or even garbled by the time it reaches the troops. The other is that in such an organization, access to and possession of information is power, and people at one level or another often simply decline to share their power by refusing to share information.

Although we are concerned about the growth of bureaucracy in a large and complex society, most of the experts believe it's an overrated problem. They argue that the rate of change has accelerated in our society to the point that a real bureaucracy would simply collapse because of its inefficiency. I also believe that while bureaucratic behavior is frustrating to the person on the receiving end, people in general are much too resourceful to be stymied for long by the bureaucrats. They almost always find a way through, over, or around the obstacles, although admittedly this is a waste of time and talent that the organization could harness for more productive pursuits.

The contemporary organization is harder to define because it is still emerging. We can say some things, however, about what it is trying to do. In general, it is seeking to simplify structure and to be more oriented toward accomplishing productive results that move the organization toward clearly stated goals. While it is often hierarchical in its structure, the hierarchy is softer and the penalties for ignoring the chain of command are generally not invoked, if they even exist.

Its major mission is to create a work environment where people can contribute something to the solution of rather complex problems. By definition, this means people need information, they need feedback, they need flexibility, and they need psychological support. In brief, they need an organization that is enabling and not restrictive.

Power in such an organization tends to be diffuse, and the organization itself tends to be much more egalitarian. Although it may be more cosmetic than real, there also seems to be greater concern for people and their problems.

Communication in such an organization is quite different from communication in the traditional organization. There is less emphasis on the chain of command (when one exists) and more on people's need for information that will help them do their jobs. Information is seen less as a source of power and more as a raw material. A major problem occurs when a traditional manager tries to behave in traditional ways in such an organization. In very short order he or she can undermine the work and destroy productivity.

Let me repeat an earlier caution. Because it is newer and seemingly more democratic, the contemporary organization, in one of its many forms, is often

31

offered as a panacea for the problems of all work groups. Yet in designing a suitable organization, one must carefully analyze the nature of the task to be accomplished. What is perfectly suitable in dealing with knowledge workers who are grappling with terribly complex and interconnected problems may be a dismal failure with people who are running a chemicals plant or maintaining an interstate highway.

It is beyond the scope of this book (and my experience) to say much more about organization per se. However, it is not the simplistic black-and-white issue that some people would like to make it.

Besides organization, other undeniable influences on the communication process are the values and attitudes of the people with whom you are trying to communicate. In this regard it might be instructive to look at the way values have changed in recent years. For example, I was born in 1932 and spent my early childhood in the last days of the Depression. My schooling was mainly during the decade of the 1940s. I went to college in the early 1950s. Over that period of time and continuing to the present, there have been some astounding value changes. Just to show how this process goes on, let me contrast what I was originally taught with what seems to be the value system my children have been learning.

As a young boy, I was lectured to on the evils of credit and installment buying. My Depression-weary parents told me and my brothers to stay out of debt at all cost. Their own pain as they struggled through those years was a vivid lesson of what it was like to be short of necessary cash. Credit buying was not very common in those days, but my parents could see the handwriting on the wall, and they knew that debt was defeating.

Another lesson my parents taught me was the virtue of consistency. Know who you are and what you believe, and stick to it. Religion, patriotism, and our dependable institutions were the rocks, they said, that you could anchor your life to, regardless of what might come. We have wise leaders who know much more than we do. So depend on their knowledge and follow them as long as you are confident that they know what they are doing. But stick with what you believe.

A third lesson of those days was the virtue of industriousness. Work hard, I was told, and your efforts will be rewarded. You will stand out from the crowd. The industrious person can have just about anything he wants in this land of opportunity if he is willing to work for it.

And, finally, I was instructed to have high regard for principles. The lesson was that principles are more important than people. You should make all sorts of personal sacrifices for a good principle, and you should be ready to sacrifice other people in defense of a principle. You should also be ready to approve of their destruction if they threaten the rest of us by violating sacred principles. Conforming to and supporting principles was serious business, and make no mistake about it: violators were prosecuted.

Like everyone else, as I matured, I learned to modify these givens in relation to my own experience and needs. Although I don't always honor the letter or even the spirit of these lessons, I am inevitably my parents' son and a child of the thirties and forties. If you are going to communicate with me and with others of my generation, you had better understand that this is the way the territory was mapped out for us. The maps may be in drastic need of revision, but your map had better be more convincing than ours if you want us to follow it.

Which brings me to the subject of the values that have been emerging for at least the last two decades. In contrast to the abstemiousness preached by the parents of my generation, the thrust of modern advertising and of contemporary thought is essentially "you owe it to yourself to get it now . . . so, why wait?" Much is made of the notion that we should satisfy our desires as quickly as we possibly can — whether that means a new boat, a new car, or a new sexual relationship. In American society a new gospel of self-centeredness is being preached with considerable effect.

That notion, always an appealing one to the individual and now being legitimized as a lifetime goal by the popular press and TV, seems to be gaining an important grip on our lives. The parent of the 1970s, unlike my own parents, has a very difficult time persuading his or her children to work hard for the future so that they can attain a better standard of living. Most of them have a good standard of living now and can't conceive of a time when they won't. With so much instant gratification of needs, it is hard to persuade people that they should postpone satisfaction of any want. And it is doubly hard to suggest that short-term sacrifice for the long-term gain makes sense.

Similarly, consistency of thought or purpose is

difficult to advocate. The one constant in our lives, says the new cliché, is change. In the face of an unprecedented rate of change, how can one hold for a lifetime to the same basic set of principles? It would be like my trying to apply my parents' formula without making allowances for my own experience and without modification. The basic principles may hold up over time, but they certainly don't hold up without revision.

Of all the givens of my childhood, regard for principles and institutions has perhaps received the worst beating. The gruesome spectacles of Vietnam and Watergate will haunt my children's generation for years to come. Their formative experience with government, unlike mine, was not a reassuring voice on the radio delivering "a fireside chat." It was protest and civil disobedience directed at a government that refused to heed public opinion until finally it had no choice. And it was the spectacle of the Vice President and later the President being forced from office for separate criminal acts.

Is it any wonder that our youngsters have become cynical in their attitudes toward institutions? They simply are unable to put such events into perspective and to escape the depressing feeling that all institutions are corrupt at the core.

Still, people are resourceful, and they cope. The result is that amid the predictable cynicism that such events lead to, we have managed to weave some emerging values to give sanity and purpose to our lives. Specifically, my parents' high regard for principles and things is being reversed into an attitude that says, "*People* are to be valued, not things or abstract principles." Almost as a corollary, the value is emerging that "the quality of *my* life is what I must concern myself with." Personal fulfillment seems to be replacing the notions of self-sacrifice and postponement of satisfaction.

What does all of this say about organizational communication? The answer is, Plenty. As Drucker says, the recipients control the communication process. Their values and attitudes determine the direction it will finally take. Their perceptions are the ones that finally count. Any kind of communication that does not take into account the value changes of the recipients will be seen by them as irrelevant and quaint. For example, the management that simply assumes that it has the respect and loyalty of its people, that the people will give their allegiance because they believe management knows best and will do what is right for them is crazy. I can think of no other adjective to describe that management's state of mind,

People simply will not respond to "because I'm management and I say so." Oh, they may respond temporarily as a matter of form, but their behavior will change as soon as the boss is out of sight. Similarly, the management that expects people to care very much about profits or productivity or overhead as gut-level issues is kidding itself. The main concern of the people is their own personal situation, and in order for them to care about these "company" issues, they had better see a clear and direct connection to their lives and their fate. If not, they will dismiss them as so much more rhetoric from management.

Clearly, people come into the process of communication with their own management with a certain degree of skepticism. Anything that feeds that skepticism or that converts it into cynicism is unfortunate for both the individual and the organization. In fact, people now begin largely from the premise of "Show me that you *are not* guilty of what I suspect you are guilty of." This is obviously a reversal of the traditional assumption of innocence until guilt is proved, but the revelations of the past few years of corporate wrongdoing have made people understandably suspicious.

On top of this, the track records of many large organizations in their dealings with their people are not very good. In too many companies and in too many institutions, people have been regarded as a disposable resource to be inventoried, used up, and eventually discarded. This disregard for human needs has been characteristic of what Robert Pearse of the Boston University School of Management describes as "the people-using" organization. Pearse claims that traditionally the key functions in a business have been production and sales operations. The important tasks have been making a cost-effective product and selling it as efficiently as possible.

But Pearse claims that things are changing. Inflation, growing shortages of natural resources, international food shortages—all spell a very different socioeconomic environment. Pearse suggests that the key to long-term organizational success is sophisticated human resources management, together with rapid innovation. In the future, he asserts, business will have to engineer some massive changes in its traditional operating methods.

Our two older organizational models—the entrepreneurial and the bureaucratic—both use people but in different ways. In the entrepreneurial model, the firm tends to concentrate its power and authority at the top. Subordinates are seen as instruments of production, like a machine or raw materials. They are dispensable and practically interchangeable.

The bureaucratic organization uses people in the sense that it provides relative job security in exchange for near total compliance with and conformity to bureaucratic norms and pressures. In Pearse's words,

> The well adjusted managers in the bureaucratic organizations conform to the restrictive requirements of the role. They stick their necks out as little as possible, and they keep tuned to the signals emanating from the shifting power centers in the organizational levels above them. There is little encouragement for the individual to take the initiative in bureaucracies; inertia and adherence to the rules are the kinds of things that preserve job security.[3]

By way of contrast, the people-building organization that Pearse says will typify the years ahead is people-conscious. What this means is that it recognizes and cultivates the very special resources that only human beings can bring to any organization. The emphasis, therefore, is on valuing and developing people for their own good and the good of the organization.

In the people-building organization, the management task is a much different proposition. Therefore, the communication task is also considerably different. If you are going to develop people's skills, you certainly cannot restrict their diet of information and expect them to grow. In fact, you must invest a good deal of management time in counseling and in the complex task of being sensitive to the spoken and unspoken needs of other humans. The management process changes considerably from pure task orientation and direction to dialog and mutual planning of the work for productive results. In the next chapter this subject will be explored in greater detail because it is both an important and a complex question that begins to suggest the real nature of the employee communication task.

The corporate manager is the most important communications link the organization has with its members. If he or she does a good job of managing and communicating, the rest of the organizational structure, including the formal media and the informal communications systems, can be supportive and can augment the individual's sense of satisfaction with communication. If the manager does a poor job of communicating, even effective formal media are virtually licked before they start, since they will portray an organizational reality that does not exist for the poorly managed employee. It is essential to understand this point, since in my judgment the key to effective communication with today's disaffected and disenchanted employee audience is, more than anything, skillful line managers.

When the chief executive asserts, as chief executives are often tempted to do, that "communication is our most important problem," he or she is really saying that "we have to do a better job of managing our people." We will examine the implications of this kind of line management communication in the next chapter.

CHAPTER II

The Manager's Communication Role

THE kingpin of any employee communication effort is the common, garden-variety manager. Whether we call this person a foreman, a department head, a supervisor, a manager, a group leader, or a head something-or-other is unimportant. He or she carries the real brunt of the communication effort in our traditional hierarchical organizations. It is through such people that the doers in the organization make contact with that organization. These people interpret and enforce the rules, evaluate performance, pass out the rewards and the punishments, act as spokesmen, and, in general, are expected to facilitate the work of the group.

As anyone who has ever held this role in any kind

of organization can attest, it is a difficult and some-times trying position. Despite the fact that the typical line manager is the primary point of contact between the organization and its people, such managers are often the most poorly trained, the least experienced, and the least skillful in managing people. The ludi-crous spectacle of the smooth senior management staff making and implementing wise policies and clever plans to be screwed up royally by marginal first-line managers is all too common.

Because of its hierarchical nature, the organiza-tion tends to force its best talent to the top of the pyramid and to leave the day-to-day leadership to the apprentice managers or to the marginal managers who lack the skill or the finesse to make it to the top. There certainly are exceptions to this, and it's not fair to suggest that all first-line managers are inexperi-enced or marginal. But it's amazing how many or-ganizations are willing to assume that their people are being well supervised and well taken care of, without bothering to confirm that assumption.

The general problem for first-time managers — and it's a problem that can manifest itself for the greater part of their careers — is that their models are all wrong. If you think about where most of us get our first glimpse of what it's like to manage people, you begin to understand why beginning managers have so much trouble in their jobs. They often are harking back to an army platoon sergeant, a bull-of-the-woods foreman, a classroom martinet, or quite possibly an unreasonable and overly critical parent. The conclu-sion we often draw from such models is that supervision means authority, discipline, and punishment, with considerable emphasis on such functions as checking up on absences and lateness, watching the length of lunch periods and coffee breaks, and trying to account for empty chairs. I've even known managers who watched their people at the exits to be sure that they came and left with briefcases to be certain their people were taking work home.

The traditional communication role of managers in a hierarchy has been to concentrate on top-down communication—in effect, to tell "them" what "they" want done. The managers' task was to parcel out work, to be certain that deadlines were met, and to be certain that people were kept busy. Obviously, I am describing an unenlightened and depressing place in which to work, but even in enlightened companies, there are plenty of supervisors who openly display distrust of the judgment, good intentions, and even honesty of the people who work for them. And, of course, that distrust is normally reciprocated.

Basically, the problem is one of an abysmal lack of understanding of the needs people bring to their jobs. The attitude rests on the assumption that people are basically lazy, that they don't like to work, and given the opportunity, they will shirk responsibility most of the time. Intellectually, most of us know that these assumptions are wrong, but there's a shadowy fellow lurking in each of us who believes them. And when we see superficial evidence of this kind of behavior, that fellow somehow takes over to persuade us as supervisors to reach for the whip.

But if the vast majority of people are not lazy, why

do we see so much evidence to the contrary? The answer, I believe, is that people tend to live up to our expectations. If we give them an environment with maximum control—lots of bells and time clocks and suspicious floor supervisors—they will work long and hard to defeat the system. If, on the other hand, we treat people as responsible adults, they generally will behave that way.

Let me relate a true story to clarify the point. The names have been changed to protect the guilty. Tarzan Lenchowski was the foreman of the third shift of Ace Products Co. He was exceedingly proud of his position at Ace, having, in his words, come up the hard way. Tarzan was more impressed by his three years as an army platoon sergeant than he was by any other experience of his life. He'd loved the authority he'd had, and for him the regimentation was the kind of world he had always hoped existed somewhere.

When Tarzan was named a foreman at Ace, he quickly reverted to the only management model he had ever personally lived with. He ordered people around discourteously, criticized their work loudly and publicly, ridiculed their mistakes, looked for little transgressions to blow out of proportion, and never gave credit to anyone.

Tarzan's eventual downfall at Ace came to be known as "the saga of the white spots." It began when one of his assemblers, a diligent young woman named Trudy, came to him excitedly with a discovery about what she thought was creating problems in her job as a welder. She had noticed that the hermetically sealed packages that were rejected by quality control and

43

returned to her for rewelding all had one thing in common. There were small white spots on their backsides. She experimented and found that if she scraped off these white spots prior to welding, the failure rate in testing dropped dramatically.

When she told Tarzan about this, he laughed at her and asked her what had suddenly made her an engineer. She persisted, and he told her to get back to her bench and "take care of your own problems."

Coincidentally, as part of a formal job enrichment program at Ace, the plant manager had taken to having coffee conferences in his office with randomly selected groups of workers. Tarzan didn't like this practice, but didn't have the nerve to raise his objections to the boss. When Tarzan's turn came to send a representative, he sent Trudy, which turned out to be the mistake of his life. She was one of Tarzan's unhappiest people, and the white-spot episode had been the last straw.

When the plant manager asked her how things were going, she offered a guarded "not so good." He pursued that comment and found out that she was upset about "the leakers" that were passing across her workbench "because she was rushed and didn't have time to scrape off the white spots."

As the conversation unfolded, he learned about her efforts to correct the problem first by notifying Tarzan and then by taking the matter into her own hands when he had dismissed her suggestions. She had gone to the quality control foreman, who pulled out the specifications sheet to show her that nowhere did it say to inspect for white spots, and he wasn't about to.

Her next stop was a prior welding operation on the production line, where she found that the very hot packages were put into white plastic cooling trays and that part of the trays often melted on contact, producing the white spots. She told the production foreman what was happening and asked him not to use the trays. He responded that the jobsheet called for using them, and that she had no business nosing around his line.

He also told Tarzan to keep her out of his area, and Tarzan dressed her down with one of his well-known tantrums. At this point, she simply gave up and when she had time, she scraped off the white spots before she welded the leads on the package. When the plant manager investigated the episode, he found that the white plastic had been causing the troublesome leaks in the packages by insulating them randomly. He also found the cause of what had become a $200,000-a-month problem.

What's interesting about this story is that it really happened. In fact, the demotivated Trudys are too numerous to count. They are victims of the Tarzan Lenchowskis of the world, who believe that their responsibility is simply to watch people and to keep them busy.

At the same time, we can't be too hard on Tarzan, for the truth of the matter is that no one ever told him that communication to and with his people was a crucial job responsibility. And no one ever trained him in the particular skills of this kind of communication. Essentially he was left to his own devices.

Even worse, no one ever gives him anything very important to communicate to his people. In fact, he often discovers important company information from the plant grapevine long before it comes to him in any sort of official communiqué.

In our traditional, labor-intensive industries this situation may be tolerable as long as we are indifferent to the human costs. But in the emerging world of knowledge work, it is suicidal. In this world, information is the raw material people need in order to perform their jobs. And because their work is often so intangible and difficult to measure, they have greater need for management reaction and dialog than ever before. The people-building organization is already exerting tremendous pressure on line managers that they are largely ill equipped to understand or deal with.

With the majority of our people now performing work classified as service-oriented or as knowledge work, first-line and middle managers must be very different from Tarzan Lenchowski. They must be planners, counselors, psychologists, communicators, and even philosophers. Perhaps consultant Harry Levinson has put it best. According to him, there has been a shift from "traditional power-oriented leadership" to "leadership by negotiation" in both government and corporate organizations.[1] That shift means that leaders increasingly will need the *permission* of their followers if they are going to lead effectively.

Levinson believes that this shift is a predictable result of the higher educational levels of today's employees. In the old days dissatisfaction with the organization was manifested through union organization, sabotage, or minimum compliance with regulations and obligations. And it was mostly confined to the lower levels of the organization. That feeling of alienation has spread to the higher levels of the organization, he asserts, and we see today's employees exerting pressure to have the organization conform to *their* values and standards. (As examples of this kind of behavior, he points to the resignation of General Electric engineers in protest over nuclear power programs or Daniel Ellsberg's leaking of the Pentagon Papers.) [1]

What this means is that the manager will have to be able to manage compromise and conflict, to balance the needs of a number of intelligent, articulate followers, and to turn their hostility into problem-solving energy. Obviously, the manager can only do this if he or she is perceived as being worthy of the followers' trust and able to articulate goals toward which the group sees reason to move.

The difficult and time-consuming task of winning and holding consent requires a person who is intelligent and sensitive and who can communicate with people. To say that it is a difficult task for which we have made little provision in our training and development of managers is to badly understate the problem.

Nowhere is the problem more apparent than in the whole area of managing knowledge workers who are engaged in time-consuming and frustrating tasks with little tangible payoff. Consider, for example, the researcher who works for months to produce a product proposal that is finally rejected in favor of a marginally better or even a superior product idea; the

47

personnel specialist who designs and conducts attitude surveys that are casually read and often ignored; the market researcher who must assess the possible acceptance of a yet-to-be-invented consumer product; the advertising specialist who supervises the production of an ad or a TV commercial whose impact can never be fully measured against product sales; and on and on. All of these people require special direction and special attention to their communication needs.

The nature of this direction and attention from the manager can be described under three broad headings or managerial responsibilities. One is work definition, another is reviewing progress, and the third is functioning as a pressure valve. Let's look briefly at each of these responsibilities.

Work definition in the modern organization is a critical task. The traditional worker in preindustrial times was a craftsman, a farmer, or a tradesman. No one had to describe his work to him. It was tangible, it was there, and he simply had to do it. The modern counterparts of these people are in a similar position. For them, work is tangible and urgent.

But most of us today are employed in organizations where work is a much more impalpable thing. We are confronted with complex problems that we must attack and attempt to solve, but the solutions are by no means clear. And even when we begin the task of problem solving, we sometimes find it hard to evaluate progress. All of this is compounded by the specialization that is inherent in any organization of any size. Our perspective gets narrowed, our concern is focused on our own little piece of the action with little regard for how it fits into the total task of the organization.

My own experience in organizational communication may illustrate the point. There are thousands of people like me hired by American institutional and corporate organizations to assist with the complicated job of intraorganizational communication. The goal is laudable, but unless someone defines rather clearly what the results should be, there can be tremendous activity with little payoff.

What frequently happens is not unlike the Gretchen Greensleeves saga I described earlier. Without a clear description of mission, people like Gretchen soon define their role as corporate journalists. In rather short order they see themselves as crusading editors or investigative reporters. The predictable result is that they are soon both alienated from and confused about what they should be doing. It is not uncommon for such people to adapt a "we-they" posture toward their own management, spend a good deal of time sulking about their lack of freedom to report "the truth," and then settle in on the safe subjects no one objects to talking about. It is an almost classic case of improper definition of work and the naive assumption that if you hire professionals, they will know what has to be done without being told.

The same sort of thing happens in almost any kind of work group we can name. Often bosses do not talk about the mission of the group to the group. Instead of establishing goals, priorities, or checkpoints, they simply suppose that everyone knows both his or her job and how that job relates to the whole task. The root of this problem is that most people are embarrassed to address such basic questions with one another. The tacit assumption is that everyone knows and that if I begin asking questions, people will simply assume that I am incompetent or dumb.

A vital communication task, then, for managers of people whose work is only a portion of a large and complex task is to sit down with those people and determine whether they know why they are on the payroll, whether they truly understand the work group's goals, and whether they are aware of what is or is not a priority task for the group. To assume that everyone knows these things is simply poor management.

The effective manager communicates regularly with subordinates on such matters as goals and priorities and keeps them posted on their individual and collective progress in meeting those goals. This is the second broad communication responsibility of a manager—telling the group how they are doing. When work is not very tangible, it becomes especially important to provide people with guideposts or checkpoints of some kind so that they know how well they are performing.

In the day-to-day transactions of business, most managers give their people some idea of what these guideposts are, but not nearly enough attention is paid to the important task of sitting the group down and saying very plainly, "Here is where we have been trying to go for the last few weeks, and here is where we are. We've accomplished this; we have not accomplished that. This is what we still have left to do, and here is how I think we should do it." Once a manager begins doing this routinely, and stimulating the dialog that goes with it, the individual worker begins to understand the problem and to see better how his or her efforts fit into the total task. Without this feedback, the group is left to draw its own conclusions about its collective performance, and an "every man for himself" mentality soon begins to characterize the people who make up the group.

In this regard, one of the most important duties of the manager is evaluation of individual performance and absolutely honest counsel to the employee. Nothing is more unfair than for a manager to mislead an individual about his or her performance—either by saying nothing or by not giving honest reactions. The motive there can be cowardice on the manager's part or a misguided desire not to hurt the individual's feelings. In both cases, people are denied the information they need to correct performance deficiencies.

The third communication responsibility of any supervisor may be the most difficult. This is the need for managers to function as a pressure valve between the organization and the individual. Do the managers buffer pressure, absorbing it, containing it, maintaining a reasonable work climate for their people? Or do they let it all out, passing along every single demand, sharing every single anxiety and apprehension they feel? This is a very important communication question because it has a good deal to do with how the work group is permitted to function. Hyperactive and

51

temperamental managers can do great damage to the people resource, often under the guise of "open communication," when they don't understand this need to be a pressure valve or when they choose to ignore it.

Let's look at a sad example of what happens when a manager does not understand his or her communication responsibilities. Ozzie Jones is manager of market research for ABC Computers, a medium-size but fast-growing producer of specialized computer systems. Ozzie's four direct reports are mixed performers. One is very strong, one is adequate, one is marginal, and one is ineffective.

Underneath it all, Ozzie regards himself as sort of a glorified foreman whose main job is to get the work out according to the deadlines he's given and to do the best he can with the staff he has. More than anything he wants to be liked by his staff and to cultivate a friendly work atmosphere. He socializes often and comfortably with his staff, and he particularly enjoys sharing office gossip with them. His likes and dislikes of other personalities in the organization are well known. And this includes his own boss, whose irritating qualities he not infrequently catalogs for the three secretaries who are also part of his group.

In general his communication style is very informal. He dislikes staff meetings intensely and will hold one only if there is a momentous event to report to his people. Most of the talk that goes on in the office is confined to the weather, politics, sports, and his particular hobby of gardening. His assumption is that his people are thoroughly professional and that it would be an affront to them to talk about goals or priorities. They know all that already, he contends.

Any discussion of group performance, he says, is out of the question because there is such a disparity in the individual capabilities of his people. Further, they all have different responsibilities, and there is no point in boring one another in talking about subjects that are not common to every member of the work group.

His marginal and ineffective performers were both very unhappy with their annual performance reviews. They had no idea before the mandatory discussion of their written performance appraisals that their supervisor was dissatisfied with their work. In one case there was an ugly scene during which a staff member proceeded to tell Ozzie exactly what he could do with that performance review.

All in all, the group is confused about its mission and the specific goals the members should be trying to achieve. They have little idea of how well they perform as a group or even individually. And they are on the receiving end of Ozzie's piques, his anxieties, his dislikes, and his temperament. Morale is terrible. There are whispered discussions about how Ozzie favors certain staff members, and despite their seeming cordiality, the members of the group long ago discovered that they don't like one another and are pretty isolated in their own job responsibilities. Ozzie is largely oblivious of all of this, which is not very surprising because it is so veiled in the phony cordiality that pervades the office.

On top of all of this, the group is badly understaffed for the job it must perform. This in turn means that there is a good deal of pressure during the work day to complete assigned tasks.

Unfortunately, that work pressure does not fall equitably on the members of the group. The poorer performers are given little to do, while the effective people are badly overworked. It all comes to a head one fateful day when Ozzie is asked to produce a rush analysis for the senior vice president of marketing. Breathlessly, Ozzie barges into the office of Ernst Vogel, his most reliable analyst, and outlines the project that has to be finished in seven days. Vogel, a conscientious and meticulous professional, sees the task as impossible in that time period. The research alone, he responds, is a five- to six-day job. On top of that, Vogel is already committed to another priority project that he has spent the last two weekends on in addition to 12-hour weekdays. The deadlines are in direct conflict, and there is no way to negotiate either one.

Fed up with the whole situation, Vogel flatly refuses to take on the new project and insists that Ozzie assign it to someone in the work group with the time to do it. That someone happens to be Ozzie's ineffective performer. Ozzie explodes, threatens to fire Vogel, and ends up doing the analysis himself. For Vogel, it's the last straw. Three months later he leaves ABC, and in his exit interview gives the interviewer enough justification to probe around, confirm Vogel's accusations, and eventually seek Ozzie's removal.

This "happy" ending is not typical in most of our companies. So long as managers were able to put out work of reasonable quality, most of them managed to hang on, almost irrespective of their ability to relate to their people and to inspire trust and confidence, which is what good managerial communication is all about. But Levinson predicts that with the manager being called on more and more to manage compromise and to balance the needs of intelligent and articulate workers, the Ozzie Joneses of the world will find it harder and harder to survive, and our organizations will find it increasingly difficult to continue to shut their eyes to the problem.

The question is: How can we get organizational managers to change their bad habits? This is not an easy matter because people in managerial positions have generally operated from a power base and from a value system that did not require them to worry about effective communication as a *business* priority. To be sure, they are human and have needed approval and affection, and this need has had its effect on their behavior, but it has been a rare organization that has told its managers that it was important to win the consent and approval of their people.

In the absence of that management value and of support systems in the organization to encourage the managers to behave that way, they typically have relied on simplistic notions of rewarding "good" behavior and punishing "bad" behavior. The rewards were generally money or increased status, and the punishments were the withholding of money and status, subtle and not so subtle personal abuse, threats, firings, and banishment to undesirable jobs or undesirable locations. To anyone who has done

55

time in an organization, this whole chapter of business history is too familiar for us to dwell very much on it. But the truth is that most of this managerial behavior is more appropriate in parent–child relationships than it is in the relationship of one adult to another.

Unfortunately, this type of behavior is so ingrained in organizations that it is not going to be changed easily. In my opinion, two things will act to change it over the long term. One is the upward pressure we have already noted from people who are determined to have more autonomy in their organizational experience and relationships. The other is the growing comprehension by management that people are indeed *the* critical organizational resource and that they had better be managed properly if the organization is to do the work society needs to have done.

To that end, many organizations have developed both systems and techniques that help them assess the ability of the manager to develop, supervise, and communicate with his people. A good example is the ongoing attitude survey. In some companies this tool has been refined to the point where at any given time, at least one segment of the organization is being surveyed. When this kind of perpetual and objective survey of employee attitudes is used, it is possible to develop norms for employee attitudes and morale and to determine and locate particular work groups whose profiles deviate significantly from both company norms and industrial norms in general. An effective attitude survey program that provides for feedback and problem resolution can be worth its weight in gold. Without such a program both the company and the manager are continually shooting in the dark. What is the true level of employee morale? What should it be, based on past experience? How do the attitudes of that organization compare with the attitudes of similar groups of workers in other companies? These are critical questions if you wish to assess the psychological health of the organization and to evaluate the quality of its people management and people concern.

One of the interesting by-products in the wake of the civil rights legislation of the sixties and the legislation that led to affirmative action programs for minority employees and for women has been the attention given to people management. Two things happened. First, management had to take a hard look at what line managers were actually doing in managing the people assigned to them to be certain that the managers were not manifesting prejudicial behavior. Second, because of the demand that minority and female candidates be hired and identified for development and promotion, management had to look closely at both hiring practices and development programs. What they saw often did not gladden their hearts. And while affirmative action programs have not been universally applauded, they have certainly helped put a greater degree of objectivity into practices for hiring and for selection for promotion.

In turn, this has led to the need for managers to pay close attention to the task of people development and performance review. In years past, organizations had few, if any, systematic procedures for identifying job opportunities in the organization and for helping people get the kind of training they needed to move to those opportunities. When these same organizations were faced with the massive task of hiring and training people whose job skills and organizational experience were seriously limited, everyone benefited. It would be naive to suggest that the programs as they actually operate in the work place are totally objective. They are still being operated by fallible human beings.

What has happened, however, is that personnel people have had to invent and establish elaborate training programs to equip people with skills they did not carry into the organization when they signed on. This is a significant development in American corporations. The other thing that has happened is that a good deal more attention had to be paid to the manager's willingness and ability to manage people intelligently and to help them develop their skills and their potential.

Viewed objectively, these are exciting developments. They are indeed in sharp contrast to previous haphazard trial-and-error systems, which required employees to learn and improve almost intuitively. Those who learned to play that game well and who had a reasonable sense of politics managed to take care of themselves. Those who were not as political or who for personal reasons declined to participate in that game did not. The contrast between the old and the new may not be as sharp as I am drawing it here, but there is certainly an important shift in the making that requires the manager to manage and develop *persons*, rather than simply to meet deadlines and manage budgets.

Clearly, organizations have to know about the impact of their managers on the people below. One straw in the wind suggested by Harry Levinson and a program actually being used by a few companies, such as Sun Oil and Illinois Bell, is the so-called upward appraisal—the evaluation of managers by their subordinates. It's a suggestion that makes a good many managers question the notion that turnabout is fair play. But it is an interesting check on managerial behavior and performance, as well as a means of improving two-way communication in the organization. And, on balance, it is probably no more subject to error and distortion than the traditional managerial evaluation of subordinates.[1]

However, it is a further challenge to the manager's power and authority. And that raises a question so far not addressed in this discussion of the manager's communication role, but a question that looms rather large. Specifically, what about the managers' well-being in this difficult role of counselor, supervisor, reviewer, and absorber of punishment from above and below? Are we asking more of them than ordinary mortals should be expected to deliver? Are we looking for a paragon of managerial fairness, good will, and all-around good fellowship? This is not a question to be dismissed lightly, since the managers' influence and performance will seriously affect the ability of our organizations to become more human and more humane.

Perhaps the best approach to this question is to look at the conflicting demands managers can get caught in in trying to fulfill their job responsibilities. Ray Dooer is a 43-year-old staff manager in personnel in a hypothetical company. He has seven people reporting to him in a specialized staff function. Three hold clerical positions; the other four are highly skilled professionals whose work is rather neatly partitioned so that they don't have many of the same tasks.

By temperament, Ray is an efficient though rather easy-going manager. He enjoys a good relationship with each of his people, although he is not an easy person to know. He respects the privacy of his people and believes that his job is to attend to their performance and not much more. One of Ray's problems as a manager is that he dislikes criticizing marginal performance. Frequently he masks the degree of his displeasure or concern with overly tactful and gentle words. His people are perceptive enough to sense when he is more dissatisfied than his outward behavior shows, and it makes them uncomfortable about their own performance. Too often the nagging question is how does he *really* feel? Where the hell do I stand with this guy?

Their concern manifests itself in tension and hostility toward one another, almost a sibling rivalry. Ray is aware that his people don't like one another too well because they occasionally complain to him about the performance of the other members of the group. Ray listens politely and noncommittally to such complaining and usually defends the behavior of the person being criticized or simply refuses to discuss it. He feels the group functions well, is productive and professional. He's satisfied.

One day Ray is notified that his staff will be part of an overall departmental attitude survey. Good, he thinks, It will be nice to confirm how good morale is and how well he's doing in managing his group. Ray is part of the survey himself, and he is happy to record his largely positive responses to the questions.

His first inkling that all is not well comes not long after the survey, when the personnel representative in his area comes to him with the news that there appear to be some people problems on his own staff and would he have any insights as to what they might be? Ray's first reaction is to recount some of the personality conflicts he's aware of and to blame them for whatever negative responses are showing up. He's urged to hold a feedback session as soon as possible with his boss and his two peer managers and all their people. Because the results are to be used for the whole department, it is felt that this joint meeting is the best way to get people to elaborate on their concerns. Ray goes to the session certain that whatever problems exist are worse for his peer managers.

Once at the meeting, Ray is stunned to discover that the people who are most vocal about their problems with morale and with the way they are being managed are his own direct reports. As the meeting goes on, he is at first surprised and then angered as he hears their words of criticism, some of it openly of him, the rest of it either veiled or having more significance than first meets the eye. Ray remembers snatches of conversation with each of them in other meetings and at other times, and he now is hearing oblique restatements of those conversations. His anger changes to feelings of betrayal.

What the hell's going on here? He always was decent and fair with each one of these people. He did the best he could for them in view of budget problems, layoffs, and restricted career paths, and now they're making it sound as though there's a rat's nest in his operation. He can see the concern on his boss's face as he tries to probe some of their feelings and insinuations.

How could they be so unfeeling and even disloyal? Didn't they have any idea of how they were making him look in front of everyone else? Ray becomes increasingly depressed as he sits there wondering how things could have gone so far without his understanding what was happening.

At one point when the members of the group are unable to articulate their problems with each other, there is a long and excruciating silence. The problems are so delicate they won't even discuss them. At this point someone suggests a team-building laboratory with a disinterested third party who can help the group come to grips with their unspoken feelings. Although they all admit there's a potentially serious problem, they're divided on whether they want to get into something as direct and confronting as this laboratory. The group decides to hold off on the team-building laboratory unless the members are in agreement that this technique will produce results.

On the way out of the conference room, Ray tries

to reassure his boss that things aren't as bad as they look. These people may be exaggerating a bit, and besides, they were more vocal because he encourages that kind of dialog. The people in his peer managers' groups would have been saying similar things if they weren't afraid to speak up. The expression on his boss's face says he doesn't believe it.

Let's stop the flow of this little scenario for a minute and determine how all of this came about. In large measure Ray is the victim of changing trends and of a tendency to depose leaders who displease the group's informal leadership. His own organizational training was with a company that invested managers with something close to divine right. There were rules and regulations in that organization, and people expected you to toe the line. Transgressions and transgressors were disciplined with dispatch. There was a high premium on conformity and obedience. In any dispute between a manager and his or her subordinates, the manager could expect 100 percent backing from his superiors for any decision or action that did not violate the law. And even then, depending on circumstances, he might find himself protected as part of the management fraternity.

Ray has always despised this system and its heavy demand for conformity to the code. It was lubricated by fear, and it depended on staunch loyalty of a highly personal sort. Ray promised himself that if he ever became a manager, he would have none of this. He would always give people the freedom and the latitude they needed to do the job. And he would never intrude on their personal privacy. None of this cowardly insistence on rules and regulations and appearances. People would be respected as honest and as persons of worth and dignity.

And when he had become a manager some years later with another company, he was true to his word. There was only one thing he forgot to do. He didn't explain himself or his motives to people. He thought they were capable of judging for themselves why he managed as he did. In fact, he felt the reasons were evident. He was businesslike and friendly in his own way, but there was little or no attempt to get to know his subordinates as people.

Not surprisingly, they marked this down as indifference to them as people. Although Ray had exceptionally good communication skills, he rarely used them with his own people. This was part training and part his own personality.

As times have changed, very few organizations have told the Ray Dooers of the world that they are in a new ballgame. There may have seemed to be no need to sit such people down and tell them what was happening and how they might cope with it, but that need was emerging, no matter how dimly it was perceived by most of us. And, of course, this is exactly the problem with so many of these kinds of changes. By the time you understand what has been happening to you, you may already be in so deep that you can't extricate yourself.

Fortunately, Ray's situation was salvaged by Ray himself and by the reserve of good will and trust that he had managed to accumulate with each of his people individually over the years. When he understood that the cause of the problem was simply that the group had not been confronting its own problems, he took it upon himself to establish a series of communication sessions in which the members of the group could begin to become more honest with one another.

How Ray managed to carry this off is an interesting lesson in interpersonal communication in itself. Briefly, what he managed to do was to get his people to talk and to listen to each other. That was no simple feat because they were very different from one another. There was a conservative middle-aged male, a young liberal white male, an aggressive, gung-ho liberationist woman, a very traditional woman with little patience for what she saw as the abrasiveness and the unorthodox attitudes of her female co-worker, a middle-aged white secretary, and two young secretaries, one white and one black.

In their first communication session, Ray insisted that they try to raise the problems they had with one another and to state them as clearly and as objectively as they could. The only ground rule was that each person had to listen and could not defend himself or herself. That very same rule applied to Ray himself as the discussion unfolded.

At first, there were hot and heavy accusations tossed back and forth. Tempers were barely held in check, but the no-defense rule helped. When there were misunderstandings and actual breakdowns in communication, an amazing thing happened. Intermediaries emerged from the group, saying, "Look, what she's really telling you is . . ." or "Hey, listen to

65

her again. That isn't what she said to you. Here's what she said. . . ." Once they began listening to one another, they also began to share and modify attitudes and perceptions.

At one point, the young black secretary told Ray that she didn't think he liked her. In the secretary's mind, Ray was aloof to the point of being unfriendly. Worse yet, he never offered praise for a good job. It was simply accepted as what she was paid to do.

The young male complained that Ray did not listen to his problems. He seemed to listen, but in fact he never demonstrated any sympathy for the difficulties of getting the job done. His attitude appeared to be largely, "Sorry, but that's the way it is. Just go back to work and do it." He didn't object to being reminded of the facts of life; he simply would have liked Ray to acknowledge that it was tough to accomplish some of the things he had managed to accomplish and that Ray personally appreciated the difficulties and the achievements.

After a number of sometimes painful and difficult sessions, the group was able to face up to its own problems with one another and with Ray and to forge a high degree of understanding of mission and of one another's problems. An unexpected payoff was a much greater degree of tolerance among the members of the group both for one another's work problems and one another's idiosyncrasies.

The story of Ray and his communication problems is one that is duplicated over and over again in our organizations, usually with unhappy outcomes. Ray was fortunate in working for a company that used attitude surveys routinely and skillfully. Lots of other managers and subordinates are not so fortunate, and the problems simmer in a stew of human relations that everyone gags on day after day.

The continuing problem for Ray and his contemporaries in today's organizations is that they are indeed caught in sometimes conflicting and contradictory roles and responsibilities. A business friend of mine who specializes in organizational psychology claims that it takes a good deal of courage and intelligence to be a middle manager today. On the one hand, the person must cultivate this open and free communication relationship, and on the other be prepared to criticize performance or put someone on probation or even fire someone. Making sure that business responsibilities and people responsibilities don't get in the way of each other is not a task for the weak-hearted or the weak-kneed. It is a balancing act requiring a good deal of skill.

For some time Ray solved his problem by keeping his people at arm's length and by emphasizing their common responsibilities to the organization. This is not an unusual solution to that particular leadership problem, but in today's climate of eroding power bases and declining respect for authority, it is not terribly effective. If managers must win the approval and consent of the individuals they are managing, then clearly they must deal with them as flesh and blood people. They must also be prepared to take all the personal risks and the occasional pain that accompany that degree of involvement with other human beings. This role is far different from the stereotyped stiff upper lip style of leadership that many of us were taught. It means involvement, it means managing by persuasion, and it means revealing oneself to others. All of this can be very threatening for traditional managers used to masking their reactions and their emotions.

Some of the apprehension goes back to the mythology of managing stated earlier that "you can be hard on people or soft on people" and that hard is better. Similarly, there is a myth that says that you can worry about business results and profits or you can worry about people. This dichotomy, as simplistic and as false as the hard-soft dichotomy, nonetheless continues to exert a strong influence over the actual behavior of a good many managers who should know better.

That open and informal communication relationships work was dramatically demonstrated in a study done at one large southwestern company a few years ago. Self-described "highly motivated" people were asked to assess their boss's behavior. The results are instructive.[2] The vast majority described the boss in the following terms:

Easy to talk to even when under pressure.
Tries to see merit in your ideas, even if they conflict with his.
Tries to help people understand company objectives.
Tries to give people all the information they want.
Has consistently high expectations of subordinates.

Tries to encourage people to reach out in new
directions.

Takes your mistakes in stride, so long as you learn
from them.

Tries mainly to correct mistakes and avoid them
in future.

Expects superior performance and gives credit
when you do it.

Obviously, many of these points have to do with
the manager's communication and management
style. In an organization that is concerned with building people's skills, that style becomes terribly important. In this kind of organization people can't be
moved into management slots indiscriminately, and
simply as a reward for their work as individual con-
tributors. It becomes much more important to look at
the whole person and the impact that person has or is
likely to have on the people he or she will manage.

What this means is a significant change in the
standards by which we select managerial candidates.
It also signifies a very important shift in the value
system of our large corporations. No one has described that shift more forcefully than Daniel Bell.
The Harvard sociologist argues that for most of our
industrial history, our business organizations have
operated in what he calls the "economizing mode." [3]
In plain English this means that they have concerned
themselves mainly, if not exclusively, with their own
profit and loss statements and their ability to grow
and prosper in their chosen marketplaces. As long as
such organizations were able to provide more and

more goods to the people as well as more and more jobs, criticism was muted and seen as coming mostly from soreheads outside the system, people who were eager to do in the goose because they received no portion of the golden eggs.

By the 1950s the corporation had established a new legitimacy for itself in American life. Efficiency, productivity, and good management according to sound business principles were touted as the reasons for the prosperity that typified the soaring sixties. But the troublesome challenges hurled at American institutions during the Vietnam war, the periodic downturns and eventual recessions, the unemployment, and the frightening specter of an energy shortage have all dulled the memory of that earlier era of euphoria and self-congratulation. In Bell's words, "A feeling has begun to spread in the country that corporate performance has made the society uglier, dirtier, more polluted, and noxious. The sense of identity between the self-interest of the corporation and the public interest has been replaced by a sense of incongruence.[3]

In place of the traditional economizing behavior, our corporate organizations are becoming more conscious of their identities as social structures, Bell asserts.

> Corporations are institutions for economizing; but they are also ways of life for their members. . . . A business corporation, like a university, or a government agency, or a large hospital—each with its hierarchy and status system—is now a lifetime experience for many of its members. Necessarily, therefore, it can no longer be an

instrument satisfying a single end . . . but it has to be a satisfactory way of life for its members. It not only has to satisfy its customers; it has to be agreeable to its "self." [4]

In sum, Bell sees the corporation operating on a continuum with economizing at one end and "sociologizing" at the other. He concludes that on balance the corporation will tend more toward the latter than the former, concerning itself with such "new" demands as job satisfaction, equal opportunity, community responsibility, environmental responsibility, and confrontation with moral and ethical issues. As the decade of the seventies moves to a close, it is hard to dispute that these are the concerns that have consumed considerable management attention and energy.

In this sort of organizational environment it is not surprising that the manager's time and attention are focused increasingly on the essential social task of communicating well with his or her people. The organization can perform that task only through its human agents—the managers assigned that task.

Such persons were described at the beginning of this chapter as the kingpins of any organizational communication effort. Let's look now at how the rest of the organizational effort can be designed to ensure that the kingpin does not get chewed up or worn out by friction, causing the wheels to collapse and the engine to be derailed.

CHAPTER III

The Beleaguered Senior Manager

IT is certainly no secret that the people sitting at the top of our organizations, in the pyramid structure we are so fond of, are in trouble. There was a time in the not too distant past when they could make decisions and be reasonably certain that the organization would respond about as they had ordered. No more.

Today they must worry about, and concern themselves with, a variety of vocal and often contradictory demands. Their hands are often tied by government requirements, by union restrictions, by the moral and legal pressures of consumer groups, by environmentalists, and by a variety of advocacy groups within their own organizations. It is not unusual for a large corporation to have a variety of organized internal constituencies with whom management must deal. In

72

addition to dealing with the labor union, the chief executive and his staff (or, in a few cases, her staff) often actually must bargain with a black caucus, a women's caucus, and a management organization of some type. And these are on top of the vested interests of the traditional functional specialties of sales, engineering, manufacturing, and the like. The people at the top often must feel as though they have been lashed to the mainmast of a ship in a hurricane. To make matters worse, the members of the crew take turns throwing buckets of water at them.

Viewing this scene, Warren Bennis, president of the University of Cincinnati and a well-known management consultant and observer, was moved to make this comment:

> Just think: At a certain point, following our current practices and national mood, all sense of individual responsibility will rapidly erode. And along with that, the volume of "bellyaching" and vacuous preaching about "the system" will grow more strident. The result: Leaders who *are* around either will be too weak or will avoid the inevitable risks involved in doing *anything*—whether good, bad, or indifferent.[1]

And, of course, that weakness or timidity is the real tragedy of our present anti-institution mood. Rather than merely making our leaders work harder or feel more harassed, it encourages them to barricade themselves in their offices and not lead at all. And, not incidentally, it encourages them to regard all forms of communication as very risky business indeed. What you say not only can, but probably will, be held against you now and in the future.

Today's organizational leader, probably more so

than at any other time in our history, must understand the events that are swirling all around him. Not
only must he understand them, he must also develop
some sort of personal perspective from which to deal
with them. Otherwise, he will avoid, defend, withdraw, and in other ways react inappropriately. This is
not to say that those responses are always inappropri-
ate, but he must respond to events as they actually
are, not as his biases or past experience dictate.

Perhaps Bell has given us the clearest formulation
of what is happening to us as a society in his book *The
Cultural Contradictions of Capitalism*. Basically, he sees
our contemporary world as an uneasy amalgam of
three realms based on three contradictory principles.
First, there is the economic realm governed by the
principle of efficiency, the ever-present bottom line.
Second, there is the polity or the state governed by
the principle of equality. And, finally, there is the
realm of culture governed by what he calls the principle of self-realization or self-gratification.[2]

Practically by definition, these three realms are in
conflict with one another. And conflict exists even
within a single realm. Corporations, for example, in
their daily practices epitomize the principle of
efficiency—minimized costs and maximized profits.
And yet those same corporations in their products
and promotion urge pleasure, instant gratification,
and letting go. Paradoxically, corporate leaders are
surprised and even indignant when such values as
instant gratification begin to undermine people's dedication to work and their willingness to postpone, to
wait for "the good things of life." It rarely occurs to

them that in their advertising they have helped further the kind of hedonism they deplore.

What is happening, according to Bell, is that more and more demands are being made upon the society for direct allocation of goods and resources through the *political* system rather than through the economic system. This results in what Bell calls "a revolution of entitlements." He says such a revolution is now underway and that the end is not in sight. To translate such a phenomenon to its simplest terms, where workers were once afraid of losing their jobs, they now expect both a job *and* a rising standard of living.[2]

All too often the knee-jerk reaction of businesspersons to the prospect of "political" allocation of goods and resources is horror and condemnation of all who would espouse such a "socialistic" solution to our problems. The trouble with that knee-jerk reaction is that it overlooks the complexity of our age as well as the problems of that age. The role of the business executive today is twofold: to be certain that his enterprise is as successful as he can possibly make it because that is basic to everything else, and to be certain that it operates responsibly and honorably in a world that is in great need of responsible leadership.

Some business executives, looking back on the values and goals of the old technocracy, with its emphasis on efficiency and technology, would still argue from the nineteenth-century perspective of laissez-faire economics that blind profit seeking is finally in the public good, and the invisible hand of capitalism converts private vices into public benefits. But such

75

dissimilar people as economist John Kenneth Galbraith and management thinker Peter Drucker see the invisible hand theory as a bankrupt view of modern capitalism. They call on the modern business leader to see the world as connected and not as atomistic. Although these thinkers travel a different road to their conclusions, they arrive at approximately the same destination as Daniel Bell. Galbraith [3] and Bell [4] see the decline of capitalism and its eventual replacement or modification. Drucker [5] insists that corporate managements must be autonomous and private rather than socialized. But he warns the contemporary manager to be public in outlook and to accept the *moral* imperative to manage the talents of individuals in such a way that society gets done what is important to our common welfare. Drucker insists that managers must make the work productive and the worker an achiever, and they must improve the overall quality of our lives.

Despite their differences, the important conclusion that all three men share is that the business corporation derives its right to operate from its ability *to serve society*. When it loses this ability or when it turns its back on this responsibility, it displays a degree of arrogance that calls into question its very right to survive.

A significant part of the business executive's responsibility to mankind is their responsibility to the people who are part of the organization. In too many cases, it is not merely the general public that is distrustful and alienated from business; the very people who are supposed to do the organization's work experience that same alienation. In simpler times it may have been possible for business leadership to go its own way, to pretend that its responsibility was limited to making and selling a product at a profit.

Today, however, the complexity of the world does not allow business leadership the luxury of such an attitude. Yet, in far too many cases, business has refused to acknowledge this complexity and has gone on behaving as though social responsibility meant merely giving x number of dollars to foundations and charitable organizations. As admirable as this philanthropy has been, it is insignificant—and even wrong —if it is somehow seen by the giver or the recipient as conscience money that relieves the corporation of further responsibility to society.

That responsibility is much broader and much deeper than the mere giving of excess funds. It encompasses every activity and every action of the company in today's world. Among business executives today there is great concern about the public's lack of understanding of business, of profit, and of business priorities. There is also alarm about the public's growing hostility and distrust toward business.

The specter that haunts most business executives, who desperately want to be able to manage their business without interference (and sometimes, I regret to say, even without much accountability for their actions), is government regulation. Yale president Kingman Brewster, in looking at the economic challenges facing our world, together with the growing power of government, stated the issue succinctly.

"The challenge," he says "is economic. Thus, if government remains representative, will it not always cater to the demands of the present at the expense of the future? . . . In short, can life remain voluntary? Or will we become dependent upon paternalism at best, coercion at worst?"

Brewster suggests that any solution to this problem ought to be based on a preference for the "incentive state" rather than the "guarantee state," for the "opportunity society" over the "welfare society." The problem is that starting from very simple premises that the poor should have enough food, that old people should be aided, that sick people should be helped, we have created top-heavy bureaucratic structures which eventually ignore the problem they were asked to solve.[6]

I raise this issue in this chapter because it represents a crucial problem for the business executive to grapple with and to help resolve in the best interests of the whole society. For him to do that, however, he will have to do something that he has largely denied was part of his mission. He will have to examine the problems we face now and will probaby face in the future, and he will have to determine what unique resources his particular organization has for dealing with these present and future problems. Despite all the fancy words that have been written over the years, this sort of planning and forethought has not been an integral part of the corporate process. Most business organizations have difficulty in extending their planning process much beyond the coming five years. In a society where practically a lifetime of change is compressed into a decade, such five-year planning cycles are inadequate.

Once business leaders do begin to come to grips with such problems and issues—if, in fact, they accept such a role as a legitimate management priority—it will be essential for them to communicate both broad plans and specific actions to their external and internal audiences. If and when this happens, I believe that the much lamented credibility problem of business will largely vanish. It will vanish simply because people will begin to see that business leaders are in fact taking seriously their corporate responsibility to society.

The implications of this issue for communication are indeed serious. What is at stake is the whole question of trust. A public—including an employee public—that even occasionally has been led down the garden path, lied to, and in some cases even hoodwinked by powerful business interests is not going to begin to believe those interests until it sees tangible evidence that it should—indeed, that it *can*.

And this is the responsibility of both management and the professional communications people who assist them: first to see that the actions are correct and then to see that the words are right for communicating those actions. So many times in the past, professional communications people have earned a reputation for sleaziness and verbal sleight of hand by their willingness to produce communications that had little relationship to the facts of the matter. "PR" has too often been a code abbreviation for verbal flimflam. In those cases where skilled and articulate people have been willing to sell their skills to misrepresent, all of us have lost something very precious: those who have been willing to misrepresent have lost their integrity; those who have been misled will lose their trust.

Recognition of this fact leads us to an inescapable conclusion about organizational communication: it is senior management's responsibility to insist on and nurture by example forthright two-way communication in the organization. Particularly in today's climate, I believe this to be a truism. In practice, however, there are far too few organizations where the people at the top let it be known that this is to be the organization's operating style. In fact, in far too many organizations (although we obviously have no objective way to know how many), top management communicates in such a way that people believe they are in favor of saying nothing, of covering up, and of avoiding the whole grisly business of communicating.

The irony is that almost every senior management person would deny that charge if it were actually leveled against him or her personally. Somehow we all believe we are pretty good at this business of communicating.

I think that Warren Bennis has gotten to the heart of the issue of communication effectiveness in discussing the qualities needed by today's leader. Communication is the means and leadership is the end. If one is truly leading people, he or she must communicate, for it is action that is the substance, the raw material of effective communication. All too often we forget this simple lesson that our actions inevitably must match our words and vice versa.

There is nothing particularly surprising in Bennis's prescription for effective leadership, but it is the sort of thing we must continually remind ourselves of. It is also the sort of thing that we must relate directly to our own leadership roles, whatever these roles may be. And it is particularly relevant to the communication responsibilities of senior organization people. This is what Bennis [1] has to say:

Leaders must develop the vision and strength to call the shots.

Bennis's point simply is that people in leadership positions must be willing to take risks and to lead based on their own vision of what the institution can and should be. One of the critical risks is in *sharing* their vision. Most of us are rather pedestrian thinkers. We desperately need someone to tell us what we are capable of becoming and to outline how we might get there. This lack of vision all too often is the cause of the hopelessness and despair to which we fall victim.

The leader must be a "conceptualist," not just someone to tinker with "the nuts and bolts."

A conceptualist must have a sense of perspective; he or she must be willing to raise the fundamental questions that will affect the destiny of both the institution and society at large. This business of asking and answering the critical questions is a crucial part of effective communication. An organization that does not ask itself the critical questions and that does not share these questions with its members tends to stagnate. Such questioning is grist for effective communication in an organization because it brings up and

81

forces the members of that organization to deal with the vital issues facing them.

The leader must have a sense of continuity and significance in order to see the present in the past and the future in the present.

Bennis's point here is that the leader must be able to clarify problems and to outline understandable choices for his constituents. This gets to his role as a communicator and especially to his role as someone who *educates* people about the problems their organization faces. Such problem definition and the selection of real alternatives are at the heart of the survival and prosperity of the organization and its members.

The leader must get at the truth and learn how to filter the unwieldy flow of information into coherent patterns.

In this point, Bennis claims that the biggest problem any leader faces is getting at the truth. Most of our organizations are so large that it is almost impossible to verify information firsthand. Instead, we must rely on the perceptions and the conclusions of others who inevitably filter the facts as they are passed both up and down the organization. From the babble that comes at the leader from all sides, he must determine what is true, and he must rework all the information he receives into truths about his organization. And, of course, he must communicate those truths to the members of the organization. Otherwise, the members are left to invent their own truths with considerably less information than the leaders have and from a perspective very different from the leader's.

The leader must be a social architect who studies and shapes what is called the "culture of work" . . . the values and norms that are subtly transmitted to individuals and groups and that tend to create binding and bonding.

Here Bennis gets at a very important point. The leader must understand the culture of his or her organization. That culture has a critical impact on the behavior of the people who are part of it. It also has a critical impact on credibility. Is the culture inclined to believe or to disbelieve what is communicated from the top of the organization? The inclination to disbelieve can be disastrous to effective communication. Inevitably, the leader must try to foster a culture that encourages understanding of, participation in, and ownership of the total enterprise or at least of as much of the total as any individual can manage. Unless the leader understands the particular culture in his organization, he has little hope of communicating his goals and values in such a way that they will ultimately be accepted by the members of the organization.

Bennis finally says of the contemporary leader:
To lead others, the leader must first know himself.

In short, he must integrate his ideals with his actions and learn the difference between the desirable and the essential. The real test of any leader, says Bennis, is whether he or she can ride and direct the process of change and, in the process, build new strengths. I can think of nothing more important to credible communication than self-knowledge and authentic behavior. Senior managers must have that self-knowledge and must recognize further that everything they do as well as everything they say trans-

83

mits a message about them and about what they value.

Perhaps the most dangerous communication trap faced by senior management is the naive belief that *only* words communicate. The truth is that words probably communicate least of all. Policy, personal mannerisms and style, decisions, significant (and sometimes seemingly insignificant) corporate actions—these are the things that speak volumes about the leader and the organization.

To the management pragmatist, these may sound like pious textbook specifications that no mere mortal can meet. But if the likes of Bell, Galbraith, and Drucker are correct in their assessment of what contemporary management is up against, these are very reasonable specifications against which we can and should measure all institutional leaders. Anything less than this will not do.

But the lamentable fact remains that a great many of our institutional leaders fall short on any scale as broad-gauged as Bennis's. It is my earnest opinion that many of the woes that now beset American corporations are traceable to managers who manage but don't lead. By this, I mean simply that they are preoccupied with the maintenance tasks of their jobs. Because of day-to-day pressures, they busy themselves with two or three easily identified job responsibilities and ignore the rest.

Typically they meet deadlines, they stay under budget, and they do nothing overtly disruptive to the organization. In the minds of a great many people, those three things are all there is to management. In too many American companies, all you have to do to get by as a manager—and this often applies even at the senior levels—is to perform those three tasks well.

But do the managers develop their people? Do they communicate with them in any consistent and effective exchange? Do they try to motivate them to be as productive and as creative as they can be? All those responsibilities have been seen largely as niceties *if* they have any time and energy left over. Not enough senior managements in the real world of business, as well as in the rest of our institutions, have made any serious demands on themselves or on their subordinate managers to respond to such things as *primary* management responsibilities. In fact, except in the most progressive companies, they have tended to emphasize the manager's role in achieving certain measurable business results while ignoring his responsibility for people development and management. Given the pressing reality of "the numbers" in all business organizations, this fact is not hard to understand.

That it reflects what could be a fatal flaw in the years ahead makes it all the more significant. Unfortunately, the folklore of business tends to celebrate the practical, results-oriented person who contributes to the company's bottom line. Whether that contribution is made at the long-term expense of the organization is rarely given much thought. The folklore is dangerous precisely because it emphasizes short-term results irrespective of their long-term cost.

To illustrate that point, let's take another look at XYZ Associates, the mythical and somewhat troubled computer company described in Chapter I. XYZ, you may recall, was a results-oriented organization in a highly charged, highly competitive business. Ron Hutton is the senior vice president for sales at XYZ. He is a youngish, glib, extremely bright man who made his way to his present position during the days of XYZ's rapid corporate growth. He began as a salesman in one of the company's regional offices and soon won the attention and approval of all of XYZ's top people. He was the epitome of the suave and successful salesman, charming customers and wheeling and dealing both inside and outside the XYZ organization.

As XYZ's business grew at an almost explosive rate, Hutton was one of the first people considered for grooming for a top position. Unfortunately, the growth was so explosive that there was never really time to move him at a planned and orderly pace through the various corporate chairs. The result was that he missed a number of jobs that would have helped prepare him for the complexity and ambiguity of managing a fast-growth company. The prevailing feeling at the time was, "Ron can hack it. He's the best we've got."

By and large he did hack it, except when the marketplace began to get tougher than it had been in the days when he first broke into the business. By the time he arrived in his position of senior vice president of sales, it was painfully obvious that XYZ needed new hardware to whet the appetite of customers who were beginning to be tempted to buy competitive products with a greater range of features than the standard XYZ line.

XYZ had had a new computer under development for close to 5 years. When Hutton was elevated to the top sales job, the technical people were estimating that they were about 18 months from product introduction. Everywhere Hutton went, he was asked by XYZ salespeople when the new computer was going to be ready. They complained that they could no longer sell against competition with the same tired products. Something had to be done.

Soon Hutton began agreeing with their assessment and working to persuade XYZ president Dave Otter that the technical people were dragging their feet. Hutton acknowledged that this was indeed a tough technical challenge but said they would simply have to cut the introduction time from 18 months to 6 to 9 months. If they couldn't meet that schedule, he had serious doubts about whether sales could meet its operating plan for the coming year.

As Hutton outlined the bleak market prospects, Otter became more and more persuaded that Hutton was right, that somehow he had to light a fire under Howard Greenfield, his senior vice president of engineering. Greenfield was frustrated by the delays that had plagued the new-product development for this particular computer, but he argued that the customer features demanded by sales imposed very difficult technical specifications and that his people "could not design new state-of-the-art products on demand."

In return, Hutton argued that there was no choice, that Greenfield simply had "to hold some people's feet to the fire" to get the job done. Otter finally issued an or-else order to the entire XYZ technical community to get the new product out the door in 9 months. It was simply too important to the sales picture for the next 36 months to permit any further delays.

When Greenfield met with his own staff to brief them on these developments, there was open anger. They all accepted the market need, but they knew that there were far too many unresolved technical questions to deal with. They also knew that unless these questions were satisfactorily answered, the reliability of the new computer could be severely compromised. Competition was heating up, but most of the senior technical people believed that the sales force could and should buy them the time they needed to produce a quality product. They did not want to settle for anything less than that regardless of Hutton's ranting and raving that they were leaning on their oars.

Because of pressure from Otter, who had been persuaded by Hutton that there was no choice, Greenfield ordered a stepped-up development program so that the new computer would be in manufacture in six months. The only possible way to meet such a schedule was for most of the engineering people to be assigned to this one project in task teams required to work 80 to 85 hours a week to complete their various tasks on time.

The pace was exhausting, with teams imposing cross-demands on one another because they were fearful of being unable to deal with their assignments until previous decisions were resolved by another team. Tempers grew increasingly short, and family life became a shambles for most of the people assigned to the project. It was clear that the new computer was going to be taken out of their hides.

As the weeks and months passed, morale sagged. The technical people were clearly in the XYZ doghouse, and many of them began to believe that the company was becoming so market-driven that there was little future for anyone who felt quality was more important than meeting arbitrary introduction schedules. It was a bitter time that even the successful delivery of the product did not erase.

The final outcome was also instructive. Once in the customers' locations, the computer performed erratically. There were an unusually high number of bugs in the hardware, causing a severe strain on the service force, who had not been properly trained to deal with the drastically different service requirements. It was a full two years before the reliability of the new machine met the high standards XYZ had set for itself.

Ironically, the machine itself was a marketing coup and helped XYZ regain its declining lead in its segment of the business. But the cost of speeding up the development schedule and the unforeseen service problems wiped out a good portion of the profit that should have been contributed to XYZ's balance sheet. Worst of all, the technical staff at XYZ concluded that their efforts would be governed to a significant extent by short-term business needs. Many attempts have been made to heal the wounds inflicted on them by the speed-up, including extensive interviewing and surveying to determine the extent of their disaffection, but they remain deeply skeptical of their own management and its ability to protect them from such episodes in the future.

Not even the eventual firing of Hutton for mismanaging this and other product introductions—a firing which the technical staff openly rejoiced at—gave them much faith in the commitment of XYZ to technical excellence. They believe that when the chips are down in the future, they will face the same kind of unreasonable pressure to release a marginal product. The damaging effects of the experience will linger for many years to come.

This XYZ escapade is a classic example of what happens when company management runs scared in the face of any real threat to the bottom line of the business. The fear runs so deep that no senior management is immune from it. The pressures that it can impose are excruciating for everyone who feels them directly or indirectly. Instead of intelligent leadership, management reduces everything to a compelling urgency that paralyzes people's ability to reason and to make logical decisions.

In such cases effective communication is impossible for the simple reason that the essential ingredients of trust and mutual concern are missing. The Ron Huttons of the world, though often operating from what they regard as good intentions, can devastate an organization by their irresponsibility. They simply fail to comprehend the difference between dictating and leading. And the irony is that they tend to justify their behavior on grounds that what they are doing is necessary for the company's welfare.

It is no longer possible, if indeed it ever was possible, for the president or chief executive of an organization to communicate successfully with everyone in the organization. He does not have the time, the exposure, or the opportunity to engage in such communication. Nonetheless he still plays a key role in the overall credibility of the organization by giving it his values and priorities and by making its systems and policies responsive to human needs. As the leading spokesperson of the organization, he must act right and live right because what he does reflects on the institution he leads.

Since he cannot communicate single-handedly, he must be sure that his managers understand the importance of their role in acting as surrogate communicators for him and in providing him with accurate reports of what their people are saying and thinking. This responsibility, he must persuade his managers, is not just a nuisance activity they must attend to in their spare time. It is the very essence of their jobs as managers. Of course, the best way for the president to do this is by means of his own example. If he does communicate well to and with his managers, they will soon understand that they have a similar responsibility to their own people.

The other dimension of the president's communication responsibility is the care and feeding of the professional communicators who are responsible for assisting him in this complex task. This subject is covered in some detail in the next chapter, but it is worthy of mention here.

In general, the first thing the top executive of any

organization must do in dealing with professional communicators, assuming that he is fortunate enough to have this kind of staff support, is to be sure they understand what he expects of them. This also applies to consultants, if the organization is too small to be able to afford full-time professional people on staff.

In far too many cases, such people are hired or engaged as consultants on the organization's communication problems, and then are simply left to their own devices without any direction except rigorous approval procedures on every bit of copy they produce. I can think of no better way than this to demoralize and demotivate a professional person of any kind.

The direction should not be in terms of "I need a house organ" or "I want a management newsletter established." That's like telling a neurosurgeon that you need brain surgery. The direction should take the form of a very complete description of the goals, problems, and priorities of the business as seen by the chief executive officer and his staff. Then the professional communicator should be required to produce plans and programs that address both the communication needs of the top of the organization and the information needs of the audience. The aim of satisfying the audience's information needs presupposes that the professional will make every effort to determine exactly what those needs are and will not simply do what the boss wants done.

It also presupposes that the communications people who are on staff or who are hired as consultants are planners and broad-gauge thinkers. In itself it may seem terribly naive to make this supposition. But if these people are not capable of this kind of effort, and if they are not capable of designing and establishing communication support programs that back up the line manager's effort, I would question their worth. There are thousands of good writers and editors who can establish slick, well-written publications for their organizations without having more than a minimal effect on the credibility or the effectiveness of the organization's communication systems.

Such people can contribute to a good program, but they should not be allowed to run it until or unless they understand fully what they are being called upon to do. Alas, in most organizations the editors and the writers are precisely the people who are called upon to handle communication. To what end we will see in the next chapter.

CHAPTER IV

Playing a Solo on a House Organ

IF you stop to think about the organization's primary communication needs and what should be its primary audience, its employees should rank at the top of the list. In practice, however, they do not. Why this is so is a reflection of the poor performance of both management and employee communications professionals through the years.

A major stumbling block is that everyone throws the word "communication" around with careless abandon. It is a rare organization problem that at some point in its evolution is not branded "a communication problem" or "a communication breakdown." Some truly are communication problems. But many more are simply disagreements or conflicts between humans who understand each other's positions thoroughly and who are at opposite poles of opinion.

Management too often operates under the naive assumption that if only I can communicate with the workforce, the problem will disappear. Once "they" see the indisputable logic and the magnanimous good will of my position, all will be well. That assumption, that wish, often leads management to regard professional communicators as a species of organization witchdoctor who can sprinkle some magic powder on the heads of the readers or listeners and get them to act and think the way the organization would like them to. In years past in this position I have even been told by frustrated corporate managers in some of the companies I've worked for, "We've got to make *them* understand." Rarely, if ever, was it stated that directly, but the message was clear.

The trouble is that the people who believe that the communication process can be used in this way see communication as merely the transmission of ideas and information from one mind to another. That mechanistic view of the process and of human relations is superficial indeed, but it is unfortunately typical of people who regard other people merely as one more resource of the organization to be expended in the achievement of organizational goals.

Communication does not mean simply telling or hearing something. In fact, never before in the history of the world do so many people know what is going on in that world. It is questionable, however, how well they understand what they presumably know. Real communication means communion, a

95

sharing of ideas and feelings, at the very least a common understanding of the problem. Within that definition, people can disagree, but at least they know what they are disagreeing about.

The problem is that this kind of communication requires experience and mutual trust and, above all, human contact. It is terribly time-consuming, and it must be absolutely consistent with the organization's day-to-day behavior. By no stretch of the imagination can senior management relegate this vital responsibility to a house organ editor and then give him or her no guidance, no support, and no authority. And yet this has largely been the shameful story of employee communication in business.

Two things are happening in today's business world that suggest to me that the task of internal communication is becoming the most important of the organization's communication concerns. One we have already noted is that the kind of work that so many of our organizations are called upon to perform requires employees who are knowledgeable and committed. To me this means that they must be well informed about the problems and priorities of the business.

The other thing is that communications people are beginning to wake up to the fact that perhaps the organization's most credible spokesmen are the members of the workforce. If these people believe in the integrity and the good faith of their employer, they are persuasive in communicating that belief to their friends, their families, and their co-workers. If they have serious doubts or if they are cynical about their organizations, they communicate *these* feelings with the authority and credibility of an insider.

Both of these facts suggest that all organizations would be well advised to develop careful employee communication strategies and to staff a dedicated employee communication function with the most competent professional people they can find. In fact, this is usually not done. The Gretchen Greensleeves saga related earlier is much closer to the reality of employee communication in most organizations.

Generally the reason for this is sheer neglect caused by management's ignorance of what an effective staff can do if it is properly directed and supported. Because the Gretchen Greensleeves of the world have developed a reputation for being house organ editors and because they normally do such an embarrassingly bad job, no one takes them seriously enough to believe that they could help accomplish business objectives. And, sadly, this judgment is probably correct in those cases where the same tired house organ (the very name suggests an anachronism in today's business environment) publishes the same tired and clichéd messages from the president, the tired and posed photos of those receiving meaningless awards (known in the trade as "grip and grin" photos), and the same endless list of retirees, new employees, and birthdays. How in God's name could anyone take such a frivolous and boring venture seriously?

The solution lies in suspending such a publication as quickly as possible, moving Gretchen back to her secretarial duties, and hiring two or three people who can plan and execute a total internal communication program matched to the business plan of the organization. (More about this later.)

The other reason that management has tended not to pay much attention to the internal communication function is that until recently, no one really expected to get this sort of communication. People were hired to do a job, and they were told what management felt they ought to know in order to do that job—no more, no less. Because business enjoyed the confidence and good will of the general public, there was little urgency to develop or even to be concerned about maintaining favorable public attitudes.

The third reason that employee communication programs have not flourished in our organizations is that professional communicators and business managers have not learned how to work effectively with one another. Often the senior manager saw communications people merely as good writers or producers of brochures and booklets and speeches, without understanding that they could be interpreters to the public of management's goals, aspirations, fears, and priorities. For their part, the communicators, coming as they so often did from a newspaper or from education, usually saw themselves as victims of corporate white slavery. They would perform, but they sure as hell wouldn't get excited about it.

The predictable result was that both parties tended to avoid each other and to be uneasy about each other's motives. The boss expected the communicator to produce an exposé and to run it in the company newspaper just before he quit. The communicator expected the boss to force him to perform all sorts of superficial and cheap communication tricks. None of these expectations were or are ever really articulated, but their existence, unspoken, is indicative of an attitude that prevails even today when both the boss and the communicator should know better.

I suppose the reason for this tension can be traced to the issue of risk and blame. In any communication situation senior management ultimately bears the brunt of both the risk and the blame. And concern over these issues has undoubtedly been reinforced by some inevitable charlatans, as house organ editors have struggled to transform themselves into communicators.

It's a bit like the story of the man who was practicing to walk a tight rope over Niagara Falls. He had decided to add a new twist by pushing a wheelbarrow with a man astride the barrow. For weeks he practiced at home on a high wire he had rigged in his backyard. His simulated man was 160 pounds of bricks, which, after a time, he could wheel back and forth on the wire with great skill. On the big day of his scheduled feat at the Falls, he stood distractedly next to his wheelbarrow, with concern written all over his face.

A neighbor approached him and expressed his unqualified belief that he was going to make it over the Falls. "What on earth are you worried about?" he asked. "I've seen you do this hundreds of times. I know you're going to make it."

The stunt man's reply was instantaneous. "Terrific! You're my man! Get on the wheelbarrow!"

Some communications people have acted similarly

with senior management. They've tried to perch management on the wheelbarrow, with considerable misgiving on the manager's part about the outcome. Communication, if it is real and if it deals with significant issues, carries some risks. There is no honest way that any communications professional can guarantee that he or she won't tip the wheelbarrow over and maybe send the boss careening into the water at the base of the falls.

Add to that the fact that the measures of communication effectiveness are ethereal indeed, and you begin to understand why management has sometimes been gun shy in its relationship with communications professionals. Management wants some reasonable assurance that any given communication effort will not lead to backlash or other undesirable consequences. The task of discussing an explosive issue responsibly and honestly is not a simple one. It requires courage to explore both the positives and the negatives and to offer reasoned argument in support of what one would hope is a reasonable management position.

Unfortunately, in the face of such a delicate communication task, both management and the communications professionals are too often tempted "to take a dive." Frequently management's out is to make sensitive subjects taboo in company documents and to forbid the communications people to print anything about them. Or, alternatively, to slap several coats of whitewash over such subjects so that no one who knows anything about the issue believes the communication. The communications people duck it with their knee-jerk reaction of "What's the use? They wouldn't let me print that anyway." With that attitude, they never even attempt to deal with issues that are gnawing away at the guts of the workforce.

The Mexican stand-off that results from this kind of relationship of senior management to its own communications people usually is the reason that Gretchen Greensleeves labors away at her nonjob, producing company social notes and insipid messages on the workability of free enterprise and the necessity for less government regulation and more profit. The fact is that few members of the workforce ever even suggested that they *wanted* government regulation or that they begrudged decent profit levels. These are the boss's itches and for him or her to scratch them with sermons in the company publication is just plain silly. It's also expensive.

John Bailey, executive director of the International Association of Business Communicators, claims that the members of IABC collectively produce company publications with a combined circulation of 228 million readers. He estimates that the cost to business of this effort is now a billion dollars a year.[1] If this kind of expenditure is going to be made, it stands to reason that business should look hard at the return on investment.

In my experience the company managements that make an honest commitment to open and full communication with their people and that back that commitment with proper staffing and resources are the exceptions. It has also been my experience that the communications professionals who truly under-

101

stand their role in the organization and who execute it skillfully are also the exceptions. There are hundreds of very skillful writers and editors who produce publications that rival the slickest of commercial publications, but in too many cases it is caviar for someone who only wanted a hamburger.

What does the audience really want if it does not want patronizing house organs or astute discussions of pending federal legislation on multinationalism or the balance of payments problem? One recent survey by Cal Downs of the University of Kansas and Michael Hazen of Wake Forest [2] points to the predictable conclusion that communication satisfaction is not traceable to any single cause, that its causes are multifaceted.

Based on their study of employees and managers from hospitals, government agencies, industry, armed forces, and universities, Downs and Hazen reported that there were eight factors that worked together to produce satisfaction or dissatisfaction with the communication system of any organization. These factors are:

1. *Communication climate:* The degree to which "attitudes toward communication are perceived as healthy."
2. *Personal feedback:* The extent to which individuals receive a direct response.
3. *Organization integration:* The individual's satisfaction with his or her immediate work environment.
4. *Relevant changes:* The extent to which employees are informed with respect to policies, goals, and financial results of the organization.

5. *Communication with superiors:* Both downward and upward.
6. *Communication with subordinates:* Satisfaction of needs.
7. *Informal communication:* Including the accuracy and efficiency of the grapevine.
8. *Media quality:* Are company media doing a good job?

The researchers stress that the most important of these factors seems to be the communication climate. If it appears that management is making an honest effort to share information and to help its people read the work environment and their place in it accurately, then people tend to be satisfied with company communication. Once again the issue seems to be: What does my work life mean, and how can I relate to it best?

Perhaps it would be worthwhile to take another look at National Bank to see Downs and Hazen's thesis in action. If you remember, National had significant problems with its tellers, who were on the verge of organizing themselves into a bargaining unit. One of the leading dissidents among the tellers is one Yvonne Yablonski. Ms. Yablonski is in her mid-twenties, and she has had two years of business education at a local junior college. She has strong feminist leanings and is a very articulate person who believes the bank's tellers have, in her words, "been screwed royally."

The chief teller at National, Esther Humdinger, is a long-term employee who simply cannot understand or deal with Yvonne. In her twenty-nine years with National, Esther has always believed that the bank's officers were men of quality who deserved her respect and her loyalty. She enjoyed her work and was especially heartened when one of the officers noticed her efforts and commended her. In fact, she sought this kind of praise almost shamelessly.

In her dealings with the other tellers, she has tried to be very motherly. In fact, the other tellers have called her Mother Humdinger behind her back for years. Most of them tolerated her meddling and her advice and believed that she was at least well intentioned.

Yvonne Yablonski, on the other hand, thought that Esther was the worst thing that had ever happened to National. On one memorable occasion in a tellers' meeting, Yvonne had taken her on personally and in front of all the other tellers called her "a tool of management and a flunky to boot." Esther left the room in tears. The tellers' meetings came to an abrupt end, and from that day on Esther has barely spoken to Yvonne.

Yvonne, figuring she had nothing to lose, next went to her local chapter of the retail clerks' union and persuaded them to form a bank tellers' division and to launch a membership sign-up drive. When the union organizers showed up in front of the bank one bright and sunny August morning, they were greeted with mild curiosity by the tellers. The officers were appalled, and panicked. An urgent officers' meeting was called to formulate a strategy to deal with the situation.

Fortunately, the bank's personnel officer understood labor relations law and very carefully briefed the officers and middle managers on their responsibilities under that law. He particularly emphasized that there was to be no interrogation of employees to gauge their interest or lack of interest in unionizing. And above all, there was to be no promise of a reward if the employees would drop consideration of the union.

A strategy was carefully developed to communicate with employees fully about their concerns at the bank. All officers and supervisors were instructed to talk informally about concerns and to try to determine what was at the bottom of all this. An open meeting was proposed to deal with the issues and even to use the bank publication, *The National Banker,* to express the officers' position. Both of those options were rejected as too risky. Instead the bank would rely on the established channels of the chain of command to communicate. The only trouble was that there really were no established communication channels.

What followed was almost comical. The union organizers, equipped with information supplied by Yvonne, kept up a steady drumbeat of arguments for joining their union. For the first time in their working careers, the delighted tellers were being wooed by the union and by their own management, which had previously ignored their concerns. One by one, the tellers accepted and signed the union authorization cards, which they were told "will merely permit an election."

At this point, Esther Humdinger decided that the

whole thing had gone far enough. One at a time she called her tellers into a conference room and demanded to know who was at the bottom of all this and if they had, in fact, signed a card. When the bank personnel manager learned what she was doing, he dashed down three flights of stairs to the conference room to stop her, but it was too late. By closing time that day, the union's lawyers were composing their complaint to the National Labor Relations Board.

Within six months, the bank employees voted for representation in the election ordered by the NLRB. As an added note of irony, on the morning following the election, *The National Banker* devoted its front page to a message from the president on the first signs of spring in the county. Included was the poem "On Crocuses," written by Esther Humdinger and dedicated to the "members of the National family."

Only those who have been a part of such corporate insanity can fully appreciate this true-to-life anecdote. Would an effective communication program have stopped the organizing effort if Esther had not taken things in her own hands? No one can say for sure, but I seriously doubt it. Massive hemorrhages are caused by pressure that builds and builds in the employee workforce. It does no good to design last-minute band-aids and apply them to the corporate forehead. The best medicine is preventive.

In this respect business communications consultant Stanley Peterfreund has done some interesting studies which show that employees who *feel* better informed hold consistently more favorable attitudes about virtually every phase of their work lives than do those who consider themselves uninformed.[3] For example, in an in-depth study of one manufacturing facility, Peterfreund reported that there was a significant difference in the number of people who agreed with a series of attitudes as compared to the number who disagreed, and that this difference was a result of the extent to which each employee felt personally informed. The results were as shown in Table 1.

Clearly, one swallow doesn't make a summer, and it's dangerous to read too much into a study of this sort, but there is at least a strong hint that communication—and specifically the perception that one is well informed—can make a difference in attitudes. In surveying nine companies Peterfreund discovered that the average employee has a rather low information quotient. Specifically, in these nine companies only 17 percent of the employees said that they "almost always knew" what was going on in the company; 54 percent said that they "sometimes knew"; an appalling 22 percent said they "seldom knew"; and 6 percent said they "never knew."

Peterfreund concludes that one of the major problems of organizational communication is that management hypnotizes itself into believing that its concern for communications is leading to actual, honest-to-Pete communication. The "s" at the end of that word makes a world of difference. What counts is the employee's perceptions, not the number or even the slickness of the publications, programs, and media transmitted to him or to her.

Shared perceptions do not come painlessly. They

TABLE 1. Study showing informed vs. uninformed employee attitudes.

| | Percent Who Agree | |
Statement	Well Informed	Poorly Informed
Management in this case tries to make employees feel a part of things.	94	63
Management tries to keep employees informed about the company.	91	57
An employee with a problem gets a fair hearing.	88	74
Employees' ideas and suggestions are listened to.	87	70
All employees here receive equal treatment.	76	54
The best-qualified people are selected for promotions.	72	55
Those who are strongly positive about the company as an employer:		
Managers	72	41
Blue-collar workers	58	30
Percent of management people who agree that the company goes all out to do the right thing for its people.	75	31

Source: Stanley Peterfreund, *The Role of Communication in Motivation* (Englewood Cliffs, N.J.: Stanley Peterfreund Associates, 1970).

are normally the product of dialog and experience. No communication media in and of themselves can accomplish this kind of human interchange. They can reinforce it, they can enlarge on it, and they can help interpret it—all of which are vital tasks in organizational communication, but there is no way that they can supplant it. And that is precisely what too many organizations are guilty of trying to do in their own communication programs. Certainly, National Bank and Gretchen Greensleeves are a perfect example of this sort of house organ soloing that allows management to delude itself into believing that the communication problem is under control.

George de Mare, one of the country's leading internal communications specialists and the author of "Corporate Lives: A Journey into the Corporate World," has been outspoken about the role that communications professionals ought to play in their organizations. He believes that they actually help an organization *survive* as an organization. In his words,[4]

> An organization, a corporation, is a community, and like any other community the people in it want to know what the hell is going on. And that's our [the communications professional's] job, because in a complex, many-faceted, chaotic and shifting community like a big corporation, neither management nor the grapevine can carry the communication load. There must be a corporate press, just as there must be a newspaper in a community or a radio outlet or some form of the press to hold the community together.

Licking his wounds a bit, de Mare admits that the establishment and operation of that corporate press is not easy: "To begin with, executives always say they're interested in communications, but they aren't. They're interested in solving the big problems confronting their organizations at the moment. If communication will help solve the problem, they'll listen."

I should add here that de Mare's generalization is mostly true, but taking it as gospel can lead communications people to a crippling case of self-pity and inaction. The secret of success for any communications professional, just as for any other staff specialist, is to help senior management solve the big problems confronting the organization. If he or she makes what is seen to be a significant contribution to that job, it usually follows that management will provide the support and freedom necessary to run an intelligent and effective communication program. The relationship between management and the communications professional cannot be antagonistic; in fact, it must be mutually supportive if the program has any hope of establishing the sense of community that de Mare correctly claims is needed.

In this regard de Mare provides some excellent advice to the communicator for dealing with senior management. He says that if you want to get management to listen to you and take your efforts seriously, you should do the following:

- First, find out what management thinks are its most pressing problems and determine if there is anything you can do about them with your specialty.
- Second, study your management. What kind of people are they? What are their interests, their prejudices, their plans and programs?
- Third, identify the opinion leaders in the organization. Who are they and where are they in the organization? What role can they or will they play in helping or hurting your efforts?

- Fourth, lie low when your specialty is of little use to the prevailing challenges.
- Fifth, get yourself trusted by assisting with the tough problems at every opportunity.
- Finally, be yourself and do distinguished work.

I would subscribe to all of these recommendations, and I would add a few of my own to the senior manager who has professional communicators working for him or her. It's an important and sometimes delicate relationship that is usually complicated by the fact that the senior manager is often a nonspecialist managing a very specialized individual. Based on my own corporate experience through the years, I would offer a half dozen critical suggestions to senior managers interested in an effective program.

First, provide free access to all company planning documents and reports of issues and problems. There is no way that any communicator can design a responsive program if he or she does not know what's going on in the organization. (If you don't trust the communicator's discretion or judgment in handling such information, you had better look for someone you do trust because your program will never get off the ground without this free access to information.)

Second, give your communications professional as much exposure as possible to senior management. Don't worry if that leads to his or her working outside your particular chain of command, as long as you are informed.

Third, help the communications professional to feel like part of the staff. Get him or her to seek the advice and counsel of other staff people in designing

111

communication programs. Discourage him or her from working as a loner. Working alone is almost an occupational hazard in the communications business.

Fourth, be courageous enough not to be upset by every little wince from senior management when a tough issue is being communicated. If nobody ever winces, you're probably dealing only with the safe issues no one gives a damn about.

Fifth, whatever you do, don't mess with the nuts and bolts of the professional communicator's work. There are hundreds of ways to get your points across. Your way may just happen to be one of the worst, and if you insist on it, you will have a demotivated staff member.

Finally, and probably most important, insist that your communication program operate from a clearly stated and mutually understood philosophical base and that it be directed from a comprehensive plan that can and will be changed as the organization's needs and problems change. In general, communications people would rather wing it as the news unfolds. If you permit them to do that, you will always have a program that merely *reacts* to events and reports them.

Let's construct another hypothetical company to see how a good senior manager can work effectively with his professional communications manager. Debbie Bower is the newly appointed vice president of personnel for Business Machines Unlimited, a manufacturer of a wide range of office equipment. She is a young and dedicated manager who has learned her craft well and who at every step in her rapid rise to the top of BMU has earned the respect of all who worked with her.

Tony Desmond, an experienced communications manager who has been doing the same work for BMU for the last ten years, manages a variety of programs, including the company newspaper, a management publication, a bulletin board program for late-breaking important news and for routine announcements, and a telephone network through which BMU employees can get answers to troublesome questions or can offer their opinions. The program has seemed to work fairly well in reporting company news, and Tony has done a good job of reporting the difficult stories that management has not always been too anxious to publish. In fact, one of the things Tony really prides himself on is his ability to uncover these unpleasant issues and events and to direct his staff in producing an acceptably laundered story that can be published, so that his management is seen as not being afraid to talk about mistakes and failures as well as successes. He believes that this is essential to credibility, and he brings to bear all his ex-newspaperman's skills to persuade BMU management that he is right.

Early in her working relationship with Tony, Debbie senses that there is mixed feeling on the part of senior management staff about BMU's policy of airing the partly washed linen for the sake of credibility. When she asks Tony about his long-range plan for communication, he gives her a document that lists all of the communication programs, their schedules, and a budget for stories to be written. She questions him about philosophy and goals and discovers that he does not believe in developing a communication plan, that he simply "keeps his ear to the ground" and reports what's happening.

Neither is she comforted by his admission that he makes no attempt to measure the success of his staff's efforts. He claims that he has done some readership studies, but he feels that they didn't tell him anything he didn't already know. "Face it, Debbie," he says, "this is a different ballgame. I can't plan and measure like other functions. My job is simply to report what's going on and to get management to give the people here honest information. You can't plan that unless you've got a crystal ball."

Tony makes it clear that he will need Debbie's support with the rest of senior management if he is to do his job. "*They* don't understand the average working Joe here," Tony says, "and that's where you and I have to get them to talk about the things that are important to our people and to print the tough stories. That's what it's all about."

Debbie has a very different view. From her perspective as vice president of personnel, she knows that BMU is caught in a perplexing cross fire of business and personnel issues that have senior management concerned about the future. Increased costs and international competition are eroding profits badly. The company's overhead structure is clearly out of balance, and some functions will have to be carefully trimmed. A wholesale cost consciousness effort needs to be carried out. BMU people have traditionally been indifferent to costs because their growth

rate has always more than compensated for in-
efficiencies that crept into the organization.

On the personnel side, BMU has fallen badly behind in meeting its affirmative action targets for
minorities and women. Recruiting is getting to be
more and more of a problem as competition in-
creases, and attitude surveys show that morale has
dipped dramatically as a result of a freeze on hiring in
headquarters operations. While BMU is actively recruiting sales and engineering candidates, it is not
hiring in other areas, and people are being called on
to work harder and harder in both the factory and
the office areas.

Debbie wants to address some of these concerns in
the company newspaper so people will have a better
understanding of what is happening to them in the
work place. She also wants some degree of acceptance
of what she believes will have to be done to make
BMU more competitive in the years ahead.

Tony is distressed by the direction he sees Debbie
wanting to go in. His main fear is that he and his staff
will be turned into propagandists for the personnel
organization and will lose their ability to report "the
warts and all." In short order the new working relationship between Debbie and Tony is breaking down,
with more and more frequent disagreement on story
ideas and story development.

Debbie is perceptive enough to understand that
the problem is that Tony and his people are almost
totally reactive. Problem number one in her mind is
to help Tony understand that there are some critical
business issues on the horizon. She begins by giving

him a copy of BMU's long-range plan. It is the first time that anyone has ever shared this kind of information with Tony. Her next move is to see that Tony attends the monthly review meetings held by the senior staff to gauge progress against plan and to identify emerging problems.

Over a period of sixty days she concentrates on giving Tony every report on the state of the business she can find. Many of these have been prepared by outside consultants and are critical of the way BMU has neglected its cost structure. In short order, Tony, who is also a very perceptive person, begins to develop a much broader perspective of the business and to share some of Debbie's concerns.

Two things occur to him very quickly. One is that BMU people must be prepared in some fashion for the inevitable belt tightening that lies ahead. If all of this happens without any explanation, he knows that the workforce will be demoralized and bewildered. There is no way, he reasons, to make everyone happy about the prospects, but at least they can be given some understanding of *why* some of these things must be done.

The other thought that occurs to him is that perhaps the best way to get at the cost and overhead issues is to involve the workforce in searching for and implementing economies. Without the support of the workforce, there is little hope that economies can be achieved short of large-scale and arbitrary cuts.

Based on his evaluation of the issues and problems, Tony begins to develop two documents. One is a statement of BMU's communication philosophy, emphasizing the need to anticipate upcoming problems and to communicate them to the total workforce. The other is a set of message goals to include the major conclusions about the business that should be communicated to BMU people. Tony's concerns about propagandizing and regurgitating the party line begin to disappear as he sees the opportunity to educate BMU people in the realities of the business.

Within a month he and his staff have put together a total communication strategy for the next 12 months. Included in that strategy is a separate plan for each of the company's communication programs so that each will reflect the message goals. Staff planning sessions are begun on a regular basis to propose and assign story ideas for the company newspaper and the management newsletter, so that each of these will be creating and developing an understanding of what BMU faces and how these issues must be addressed.

In a parallel effort, Debbie's manager of training and development begins working with Tony to determine whether there is a practical way to train BMU managers to communicate these kinds of subjects in a rational and effective dialog with their people. The result is a custom-made training course that will be given to all BMU managers so that they can learn and practice the behaviors they will need to encourage open and nondefensive communication.

Under Debbie's direction a total effort is begun to plan and measure the communication climate and program at BMU. From a reactive posture of "*They* won't let me tell the people the truth; therefore, I

117

must disguise it and release it in small, nonthreatening pieces," Tony has been converted to the role of proactive communication—a role that will allow BMU to anticipate and to defuse otherwise explosive issues.

One might well squirm a bit and challenge such communication as manipulative and 1984-ish. I disagree. At its best it permits the individual member of any organization to read the reality of his or her life and to make whatever adjustments are possible. It's much easier to cope if you know what you are up against. At its worst this sort of communication can be used to distort and confuse. In the long run, I don't believe that can work. Hypocrisy is just too hard to sustain. The liars get trapped in the day-to-day realities that everyone experiences, and in the process lose their ability to lead, simply because no one will follow. The results are usually disastrous.

Those in positions of organizational power who deliberately lie to their people (and in my experience that is a remarkably tiny fraction of the total) forget the simple fact that they are not the sole source of information. There is always an active grapevine. There is always the probing and skeptical outside press playing its rightful role. And, above all, there is the reality of one's own experience and the human tendency to reflect on and interpret that experience.

As an aside, the existence of all of these other information opportunities makes the elaborate approval routine present in some organizations doubly ludicrous. Anyone in the communications business who has had his or her copy restructured, revised, repunctuated, and rehashed for "just the right effect" by middle managers with sweaty palms has to chuckle when the local reporter or TV newscaster chucks it all for his version of the situation. Or when the grapevine irreverently chews up the message and reduces it to the corridor speculation that the message, with its guarded and official language, was supposed to prevent. Or, perhaps worst of all, when someone produces a clever parody for everyone's amusement.

My real point is that Tony and Debbie exemplify the kind of working relationship that can make the professional communicator a contributor and not an organizational parasite whose role no one quite understands. To achieve that happy state, however, it is necessary first to have a communication philosophy and a communication plan, and then to translate both of these into believable and relevant descriptions of the reality of the particular organization.

Let's consider for a moment the subject of an appropriate communication philosophy for a contemporary organization. What should you tell to whom? And when and why? These are critical questions, and the answers will probably vary somewhat from organization to organization depending on the operating style and the values of that particular organization.

In general, however, there do seem to be some universals that apply to organizational communication and that are a product of the implicit relationship of the organization and the individual. This relationship looms especially large in our time because so much of our work is done within large, complex, bureaucratic organizations. If we truly believe in the

119

dignity of the individual and in his or her need for freedom and self-respect, we cannot dismiss this relationship with a cynical shrug of the shoulder. The "that's-what-we-pay-them-for" school of thought is not just morally bankrupt—as a practical way to manage today's worker with his greater self-awareness and desire for personal fulfillment, it simply does not make sense.

Instead of house organ soloists, contemporary management should be establishing and supporting employee communication functions dedicated to the following fundamental concepts: (1) the line manager, not the professional communicator, is the primary and preferred source of information and interpretation for his or her people; and (2) the individual at any level of the organization will be most productive when the primary needs for job mastery, predictability, and recognition, appreciation, and trust have been fulfilled. These contentions are consistent not only with human needs but with the mass of modern business studies.

The role of the employee communication function should be a combination of staff support and service. The *staff* role consists of giving professional counsel to line managers, to help them identify and perform their communication roles. The *service* role consists of the mass communication programs that communications professionals actually produce.

For the people in an organization, it is important to realize that most communication is humble, short-range, and close to the daily grind. To most of them the communication problem consists of their not knowing how the boss or the company wants things done, of their not having access to necessary information, of their not having heard about changes of direction, of their not knowing management's intentions about matters that affect their (and their families') lives.

If the line manager does his or her job well in dealing with these daily concerns, and if the professional employee communication staff addresses the larger issues effectively, the people in the organization at least have the opportunity to understand their work lives and to deal with the reality of those lives. This approach is not without its problems:

- The human need for information is almost insatiable, so that whatever is provided will probably be perceived by the audience as inadequate and insufficient. (This is a fact of life and not an argument against communication.)

- The anti-institutional climate in American society today is very strong, so that a certain amount of audience skepticism (and even hostility) is inevitable.

- There has always been misgiving in corporations and other institutions about the employees' "need to know" and a tendency to tell them only those things they clearly must know to do their job. That attitude must be reexamined and altered so that only information *that must be withheld* for valid business reasons is denied the employee. The only kinds of information that should be routinely withheld are proprietary product information, closely guarded business strategy, or information bearing on another employee's right to privacy.

These matters of an unsatisfiable desire for information, anti-institutionalism, and the whole question of the employees' need to know are frustrating to both senior management and the professional communicator. What they really argue for, however, is well-thought-out programs with realistic goals. Such programs see the ideal organization not as a management-labor arena for adversary confrontation, nor as a competing ground for numerous rival pressure groups, but as an organic entity in which each individual is related to the common purposes of the whole organization.

This view differs sharply from the nineteenth-century notion of managerial autocracy that many of us have been raised with and conditioned to in our traditional organizations. It regards the self-defined well-being of the individual as one of the common purposes being served, it recognizes the legitimacy of the individual's role in contributing to and influencing decision making, and it accepts absolutely the ethical principle that people must be free to decide for themselves exactly what ends they are serving and what means they will consent to use.

I am sure that the foregoing arches the eyebrows of corporate traditionalists and sets them to gnashing their teeth, but I believe that it expresses the needs and the desires of the people, who, after all, make contemporary organizations work. The manager can no longer see himself or herself behind a microphone addressing an audience. Today the experience is more like being part of a noisy crowd, in which one must gain a hearing on the basis of merit and persuasiveness, rather than of a superior position or a stronger voice.

If this is a correct metaphor for the predicament of today's organizational managers, what are the responsibilities of the professional communications people in helping them out of that predicament or at least making them more effective in coping with it? I would cite four distinct responsibilities:

- First, to educate and support managers in the technique of communication with their people.
- Second, to provide innovative and flexible communication programs that give people the information they need as members of the corporate community.
- Third, wherever possible, to detect and clear away obstacles to communication.
- Fourth, to press for release of information needed or wanted by the people of the organization.

This last point calls for an explanation. I'm not suggesting that a communicator should behave like a journalist, pressing always for the facts that aren't offered. There is, however, a genuine need for people to know how the company is doing in the laboratory, the factory, the marketplace, and the financial community. Such information has a direct bearing on their jobs, and the communicator should try to identify it and press for its dissemination.

The arena I'm describing is no place for the slow-witted, the faint-hearted, or the cynical. The job is tough and demanding, with high visibility and considerable risk. And it requires taking positions and raising questions that senior people would sometimes much rather avoid.

Yet this job is of the utmost importance. George de Mare has stated it best:

> Communication affects everyone—both executives and employees—as human beings rather than as workers. It is more important in some ways to them than goals, skills or any single component of the whole, because it affects the way people live and see themselves during the 40 or more hours they give each week to their work. So what [the communicator's] job does—and its overriding value—is that it affects the style of life in an organization.[4]

Let's look next at some further implications of this life-style question as we examine the important matter of how we communicate *individually* within our structured organizations and what that communication means to us as autonomous people.

CHAPTER V

The Core of Credibility

ONE of the disturbing things about communication and credibility is that we often discuss them as isolated processes or natural phenomena. Often they are viewed in about the same way as we view the force of gravity. They are simply there, with little relationship to what *we* do or do not do. We know that there are techniques to enhance them and that there are strategic and tactical mistakes that can harm them.

But all too often we miss the essential point that effective communication and credibility have a highly personal component and that they are closely related to our own behavior and our own values. Perhaps the clearest object lesson on this point was the Watergate mess. The active participants in Watergate saw little, if any, connection between their behavior and the national scandal that followed that behavior. It was just plain dumb luck that they were caught doing what everyone else had been doing for years. At least that's what the apologists said and are still saying.

The insane premise is that you can behave and believe about as you please without worrying about the consequences of your behavior or your beliefs. "Insane" is not too strong a word here for the obvious reason that when words and actions bear little relationship to one another, we create a disordered and deranged situation that confounds people's ability to understand. What seems to be and what is are simply too far apart for a rational and ordered mind to deal with.

It seems to me that this matter of matching our personal behavior with our beliefs is a particularly important issue within our various organizations. The work place is important to all of us. We spend large portions of our lives there. We invest a good deal of our emotional energy there. Unfortunately, most of us are not very good at reading and understanding its reality.

Instead, we are fooled by appearances and myths. Because of its very complexity, the organizational environment is difficult to grasp. One of the problems here is that each organization tends to invent for itself a kind of organizational dogma to describe itself and to serve as beliefs that we are expected to subscribe to if we are part of the organization. Some of this dogma is well articulated and clear and almost unchangeable. Corporate organizations, for example, describe themselves as efficient, well-managed entities dedicated to serving the needs of customer, shareholder, and employee. They also paint themselves as being appreciative of and rewarding individual dedication, competence, and performance. And they claim to be dynamic and receptive to change.

The extent to which they individually and collectively measure up to these ideals is another matter. But here again we are ill prepared to deal with the reality. Our reaction to shortfall is cynical. We are not charitable enough to believe that the examples of injustice and ingratitude that we see are generally exceptions and that in most cases people do try to live up to the ideals. Instead we retreat to a cynical posture, so that we don't have to run the risk of further disillusionment or further disappointment. It is easier to assume that "they" are hypocrites and liars and that for our own good we should not believe them.

Other parts of the self-described organizational dogma are tentative and changeable. They depend on the problems the organization is grappling with at any particular time. To a certain extent these are the "fads" that all organizations fall victim to in order to solve pressing problems. That they are pronounced as dogma tends to make people even more skeptical as time goes on. Yesterday it was automation; more recently it was the conglomerate movement or multinationalism or one of a score of other organizational priorities, which become part of the announced dogma. Since they fade with time, they tend to encourage an attitude that "this too will pass" if we wait long enough.

127

Because life in our organizations tends to have these built-in instabilities and because today even some of the basic assumptions about an individual's obligations and rights within the organization are being challenged, the matter of personal communication and personal credibility is all the more significant.

Yet personal communication is largely affected by how one feels about his or her position in the organization. Is he or she afraid? confused? insecure? unable to separate the real threats from the imaginary threats? If this is the case—and all too often in our major organizations from corporations to universities to the church, it is—it is difficult to deal with the question of one's own credibility in any objective and rational way.

Volumes could easily be written on the fascinating subject of one's freedom in an organization, so complex and dim are the forces that influence people's work behavior. Most of us tend to write off such questions and to retreat to the position that existentialist Jean-Paul Sartre has called "bad faith." To put it in its most basic terms, bad faith is to pretend that one has no choice when, in fact, the choice is merely a painful one. It is evasion and running away from agonizing choices. Bad faith manifests itself in hundreds of fictions we invent for ourselves in difficult situations. What could *I* do? What would *you* do? It would have meant my job if I said no. What *choice* did I have?

The examples are all around us. They are commonplace, and they are catastrophic. The business executive overseas who pays the bribe and says, "What could I do? It was that or no contract." The salesperson who kicks back to the purchasing agent and says, "That's the way business is done. If I didn't do it, my competitor sure would." The politician who sells his vote to the highest bidder, "Look, I don't like it either, but what can you do?"

Or Adolf Eichmann at his trial, "I was obeying orders. I am a soldier." Or Lt. Calley at MyLai, who said the same thing. Or the kit and kaboodle of Watergate conspirators in chorus. "Look, it was a matter of national security. We had no choice. Those leaks had to be stopped. Besides, everybody has been doing that for years."

But, of course, the startling truth, if we examine it carefully, is that there is indeed a choice in every one of these cases if we have the courage to make it. An important complicating factor is our willingness to accept certain roles. It is not even that difficult to identify with a man like Eichmann and the horrifying acts he committed if we accept that he was a soldier and that a soldier *must* obey orders. It is perhaps true that there is no choice within that rigid role of soldier. But the individual always has the choice of stepping outside the role and reclaiming his or her freedom to act. In fact, the bad faith that Sartre speaks of is really an attempt to escape the reality of freedom.

What does this have to do with communication and personal credibility? I believe it is the core of the matter. We cannot communicate authentically without personal freedom and without valuing our own integrity. If this is so, why don't the compromisers of the world simply declare their freedom and do the right things for themselves and for their leaders?

The question is almost, but not quite, rhetorical.

The answer is partly that they value other things more than their freedom. But it is also partly a matter of misunderstanding. Most of us are terribly naive about our organizational relationships. It is so much simpler to accept the packaged truths of organizational dogma that tell us that if we work hard and keep our noses clean, we will be rewarded. It is simpler to believe that if we are loyal, the organization will return our loyalty and love us as we love it. It is easier to believe that we have a well-defined role to play within our nice, neat, rational organization.

And, of course, once we begin to question this dogma, it is infinitely easier to retreat to cynicism and alienation. However, this is still a role, which restricts our freedom and dims our powers of observation and insight. Instead of believing and contributing, we disbelieve and do as little as necessary.

Somehow we must learn how to read the truth of our organizations and to respond intelligently to that truth. But doing this will take a good deal more sophistication, patience, and charity than most of us have heretofore shown. It's also going to require us not to lapse into bad faith, in which we insist on playing roles that minimize or eliminate the tough personal choices.

The other obstacles to understanding our organizations besides bad faith and our lack of sophistication have much to do with what we see as our self-interest. It is difficult to be free within any organization if you are driven by your own ambition to seek positions of power and status. The desire for personal wealth or for the power to decide important issues has a way of leaving us wide open to all kinds of external control of our behavior. We become fearful of offending others whom we see as powerful. We court the approval and support of such people because we believe they can move us toward our goals. We become paranoid about those whom we see as our enemies in the organization. All in all, we can be easily manipulated, voluntarily transferring the strings that control our actions from puppeteer to puppeteer.

If it is not ambition, it may be a deep need for the approval of others that distorts our behavior and limits our freedom to act. Or it may be our cowardice—our deep fear of what others can do to us if they disapprove or disagree. Few people in any kind of organization escape these controls and anxieties.

And, of course, not all of these fears are unfounded. Whether you are an educator, a churchman, a corporate executive, or a civil servant, you are vulnerable to some rather frightening prospects during the length of your organizational career. Free or not, courageous or not, you can still be done in by office politics and intrigue, you can still be the victim of hard times for the organization, you can still be put on a shelf, or you can fall temporarily or permanently out of favor and be exiled to an organizational Siberia. All of these possibilities exist for all of us who cast our lot with the church, the corporation, the university, or any other organized element of society set up to achieve certain goals or missions.

The real question, it seems to me, is: How do we respond to these organizational possibilities?

Do we become office conspirators, hatching schemes and plotting for our personal benefit on the premise that that's how you make it in business? Are we willing to climb to power positions over and around the dead bodies of our victims? It's not hard to engage in the bad faith game here and to assert, "I had no choice. He (or she) was simply obstructing and refusing to budge. What could I do?"

Do we live with an unacknowledged but nagging anxiety about our prospects for the future? What if the company falls on hard times? What if overhead has to be cut? What if there are layoffs? What if they consolidate operations? Can I hang on?

Or do we fear the day of that fateful realization that we have come to the end of the road in our careers? The vice presidency will never happen, the promotions are over, and all that's left for us is to play out our careers right where we are, with the same routine and the continuing lack of challenge.

Or perhaps we are dreading the worst situation of all—the fall from a powerful position. The glories and the successes of the past are over. We are too old, too experienced, too burned out to contribute anything more, so we are shown the door by someone who believes once again that there is no choice. It has to be.

Any person who is preoccupied with these organizational possibilities is unlikely to be able to communicate effectively and credibly. Too much of this person's life is sham and pretense for him or her to be able to relate in any authentic way with other human beings.

Author Peter Berger offers sociological models of society that cast some light on the organizational dilemma that the individual faces in trying to establish his or her freedom.[1] One view is of society as a prison in which we are coerced by social institutions, by law, and by conventional morality as well as by the circumstances of our birth. In such a model, we are assigned certain behavioral boundaries that are determined by where we were born, what class we belong to, how much education we have, the racial or ethnic group we belong to, what we do for a living, and a variety of other variables largely out of our control. Berger notes that the law and the morality of society can produce elaborate justifications for each one of these sanctions, and most people will approve their being used against us as punishment for acts of rebellion.

Obviously, this is a very pessimistic model, but it is a common perception of those who have been punished by society or denied the full range of opportunity their talents might seem to justify. An extreme example would be the subservient social role of the black American until very recent years with the traditions, the conventions, and in some cases even the laws of white society being used to imprison blacks within the larger white society.

The same view of society and its institutions as a prison can also infect people who might not be seen by others as prisoners. Certainly the wealthy Boston Brahmin described by John Marquand in *The Late George Apley* was in his own peculiar way every bit as much a prisoner as a southern black. The chief difference was Apley's wealth, but his freedom to act was certainly severely limited.

In similar fashion people in organizations frequently see themselves as prisoners of the system. They fear that if they act in what is seen as an unconventional way they will be punished. An excellent example in most hierarchical organizations is the assumption that people must aspire to leadership positions or they lack initiative and ambition. The result is that in most organizations what passes for career planning is really planning for promotion to responsible positions for which the candidate may have neither the talent nor the desire. The situations that Laurence Peter describes in his explanation of the Peter Principle would be funny if they weren't so accurate and if they didn't take such a significant toll in preparing people for positions they can't handle.

In my career, one of the early fears I had to work hard to overcome was the suspicion that it was dangerous to take positions and to express my opinions publicly. In twenty years in American corporations I had stumbled on a fairly long list of truths that ran counter to the corporate dogma that people preached at me for most of this period. The discovery of these truths was always exciting and liberating for me. I reasoned that if I had been struggling with these questions, there must be thousands of others doing the same thing.

That thought led me to a near compulsion to write about some of my perceptions, particularly those that seemed counter to the conventional truths of the dogma. And yet, my concern was how would the traditionalists feel about my views? Such questioning is often unwelcome. Would I be seen as a heretic? Would I be punished in both open and subtle ways for daring to question the reality that people who saw themselves as older and wiser than I had lived by?

As I prepared my first manuscript for publication, I found myself thinking back to all the times when someone had looked at me with piercing eyes that asked, "Do you really believe that? Do you understand how dangerous that view is?" They never actually said that, but it was written all over their faces.

Perhaps the first time I ever encountered this fear in the flesh was when I was in graduate school at Albany State College for Teachers and trying desperately to drop an insulting and mindless course on the theory of audio-visual instruction in the classroom. I had signed up because I was heading for a teaching career and thought that it would be wise to know how to run a film projector and the like. To my amazement the instructor droned on and on about things like the advantages of field trips and the history of chalk boards. Everyone seemed to listen as though he were Einstein explaining the theory of relativity in layman's language. Some even asked questions.

My advisor signed my request to drop the course, but he explained that the head of the education department would also have to approve. The two of us walked to his office to obtain what I believe we both thought would be a routine approval.

The department head listened solemnly as my advisor explained why I wanted to drop the course, and then he fixed his gaze on me as I explained as earnestly as I could that this was not the course I bargained for and that I wanted out. I quickly began to suspect that I was in trouble when he called for my file and began examining my undergraduate record from Hamilton College, a small liberal arts college for men. Compared to the state college it had been Nirvana, and I appreciated it more and more as the days passed.

His first question was, "Why is it that you people from liberal arts colleges feel that you don't need to take *our* practice teaching?" I had completed practice teaching as a college senior under a high school social studies teacher who, literally, was a master teacher. I told the department head so, only mildly puzzled that we had wandered from the subject at hand to an examination of my credentials, attitudes, and expectations. It was the first time that I had seen firsthand the outraged administrator defending the system against a potential heretic. Very quickly the conversation took on an ugly overtone that I should go back to that class and pay attention because there were people lots brighter than I who felt that this was an essential course. He had no intention of signing this form, and he considered the matter closed.

When I asked him if there were any appeal route to his decision, he fixed me with a steely glare and said that I could take the matter up with the director of graduate studies, but that he would personally oppose my request. I was frustrated and angry when I left his office with my advisor. In my mind there was no choice but to escalate the matter.

While the adrenalin was still flowing, I walked

across the hall to the director's office and explained what I wanted to do and why I had come to him. He asked me no questions and silently signed my form to drop the course. When I left his office, it was with the sinking feeling that I had achieved what I set out to do but that somehow the system would find a way to reach out and deal with me. I had fantasies about the department head blackballing me for jobs and otherwise making my graduate program unpleasant, but none of that happened. I made the happy discovery that you could confront the system responsibly and calmly *if* you knew what you were talking about and *if* you were capable. That's an organizational insight that I have reaffirmed over and over again in the years since that experience.

At the same time I have often confronted my graduate school adversary reincarnated in a variety of other persons and settings. I always know him by the indignation he feels and by the anger he expresses so as to intimidate anyone who would question the reality he seems to believe in so staunchly. I must admit that he still scares me, as a cornered rat would scare me, but I know that he must be confronted for the sake of our collective sanity.

Just how far that fear can take us was brought home to me when I was working on the manuscript for my first book. The book was more than mildly critical of the corporate system. As I wrote, I wondered if it would not be prudent to publish my book under a pen name. The message would be the same, and I would not run the risk of making my superiors angry.

I was particularly concerned about my boss at that time, a man I liked and very much respected. My fear was that he would disagree with what I had written and would advise me that for my own good I had better forget it. At best, I thought he would tell me it was "my funeral." At worst, I feared he would forbid me to publish it. The result was that I continued writing it in my spare time, but I avoided showing him the manuscript or even telling him that I was writing a book. As the publisher's deadline got closer and closer, I had to make a decision about whether or not to use my own name.

After a good deal of agonizing, I knew that I had no choice. If what I was saying was true and if I really believed it, I had to sign it with my name. There was no other way.

On a Friday afternoon, with the manuscript due at the publisher's the following week, I handed my boss a copy and asked him to read it over the weekend if he possibly could. He expressed considerable interest in my doing something as ambitious as this on my own, and he promised to review it by Monday.

Because he was rather traditional in his thinking, I was apprehensive all weekend that he would misunderstand what I was trying to do. By the time I got to the office the following Monday, I had worked myself into a state, wondering how I could withdraw the whole project if he disapproved.

When I reached my office, my secretary told me that my boss wanted to see me *as soon as possible*. In the elevator, I began mentally reviewing the parts of the book I would be willing to alter. I also began drawing

138

the line that I would refuse to cross in making revisions.

As I entered my boss's office, I could feel my heart begin to race. I was a wreck as I waited for his verdict. He handed me the manuscript and said, "You know, this is really good. Somebody should have said this years ago."

I was dumbfounded. He didn't want me to change a word. Once more the lesson had been driven home. You *can* criticize the system, you *can* challenge if you do so responsibly and rationally.

In this connection, another model Peter Berger offers of society is that of a stage populated with actors. This model does not deny that the actors on the stage are constrained by the external controls set up by the playwright and the director and by the internal restraints of the role itself. But, Berger points out, the actors have the option of playing their parts enthusiastically or sullenly, of playing with inner conviction or with "distance," and sometimes of refusing to play the role at all.[2]

From that vantage point, it is clear that every social role can be played knowingly or blindly and that every social institution can be an alibi and the cause of our alienation from ourselves and our freedom. But *some* institutions at least can become protective shields for the actions of free men and women.

In our more honest moments, most of us would agree that life has its full measure of terror. To a large extent society is our defense against individual and collective terror. The routines, the rituals, the rules of our various institutions provide us with a feeling of well-being, a sense of identity, a defense against the naked terror we would experience if we were all alone and we had to deal daily with our own survival. We have constructed this world for good and necessary reasons, but we must be certain that it does not become so much of a reality to us that it obliterates who we are and what we must become as individuals.

The ideal is for us to live and work within these institutions we have created but never to allow them to dominate us. According to Berger,

> Whatever possibilities of freedom we may have . . . cannot be realized if we continue to assume that the "okay world" of society is the only world there is. Society provides us with warm, reasonably comfortable caves in which we can huddle with our fellows, beating on the drums that drown out the howling hyenas of the surrounding darkness. "Ecstasy" is the act of stepping outside the caves, alone, to face the night.[3]

In *Up the Organization*, a book that too many people thought was merely a wise guy's slap at organizational ritual and practice, Townsend says about the same thing. In the introduction, he wrote that the solution was "nonviolent guerilla warfare to dismantle our organizations where we are serving them, leaving only the parts where they're serving us." [4]

I believe that to be an authentic communicator, you must first be an authentic person, both inside and outside the organization. There are those who try to live split lives, being one sort of person at work and another sort outside of work. The strain of that kind of double life is enormous, and it probably is not possible to sustain it over the long run.

What I am suggesting is that we work *within* the system but work *against* its inhumanities and its indifference to human dignity, wherever we detect that indifference. This is a tall order that requires personal courage and sometimes putting one's principles ahead of one's personal advantage, but the payoff is twofold. One, you establish your personal freedom to act responsibly within your organization. Two, you reinforce the organization's responsibility and also its willingness (if we can speak of "the will" of a system) to serve as a protective shield for free men and women.

At this point the cynical reader may question the sanity of that kind of action. The only answer I can offer is that much depends on your own value system. Those who believe that their self-interest and their personal ambition demand that they conform and that they give themselves totally to the organization—those individuals pay an enormous price. And only they can determine whether or not it is worth it.

What makes it all doubly difficult is that the choices are rarely dramatic, like the kinds of confrontations between good and evil that we read about and see portrayed in movies and dramas about organizations. The choices are usually much more subtle and much easier for us to rationalize away to ourselves.

To be credible individuals within an organization, we must be able to step outside the cave, to examine the darkness outside as well as the darkness within, and to understand and communicate what we understand. For the truth is that a judge can and sometimes must resign, that a soldier can and sometimes must refuse to obey an order, and that any organization man or woman can and must resist mindless systems or policies that rob people of their humanity.

Otherwise, how can you trust such persons and how can you believe a word they say?

CHAPTER VI

The Siege Mentality

IF the core of organizational credibility is the honest and feeling individual, his or her opposite is the hardened and skeptical soul who believes only in the numbers. If this person cannot measure something, then it simply does not exist.

As values and attitudes change in this country, the hardened business type is more and more out of sync with both the times and his organization. Public hostility, the government regulation and investigation that are often manifestations of public hostility and distrust, and consumer agitation come at organizational leadership from all sides. In many cases that leadership wants nothing more than to be left alone to be able to deal only with the pressing problems of the business without interference by the public.

In large measure this attitude reflects the classical business creed that the business leader's role toward society is fundamentally a passive one. Essentially he is concerned with the task of making his enterprise as successful as he possibly can. If he does that well, everything else is taken care of by the dynamics of the marketplace. The customer buys or does not buy. The competition beats him or does not beat him. There are few realities beyond those in his thinking.

If we think in terms of a continuum, at one extreme would be this classical breed. At its *middle* position would be the notion that management is the *agent* for balancing the specific and sometimes competing interests of shareholders, employees, customers, and the general public.

At the other extreme is the emerging belief that management is responsible to society at large. As the industrial revolution has worn on and as the big corporation has evolved and become increasingly sophisticated, this middle position has gained increasing acceptance. And with it has emerged a professional management group to make the plans and the decisions that would see that all these interests were properly balanced.

In recent years as the general populace has come to recognize a potential conflict between its own interest and the private interests of large and powerful organizations, the inevitable question has been asked: By what authority do you who manage these huge corporations exercise your power? And what means does the public have to ensure that that power will be exercised for the general good and not simply for the enrichment of your organization?

Unfortunately, the answer from business as well as from other large and powerful organizations has been, "Trust me." In an earlier and less jaded age, that answer was accepted. But, of course, the people who accepted the answer were part of an earlier American tradition that presumed that the common good would be served by responsible leaders who would not abuse the privilege.

A necessary foundation for this particular view was the commonly held belief that people, in serving the common good, must obey the rules, they must be loyal to their government and their institutions, and they must accept discipline. These three principles of authority, loyalty, and discipline were fundamental to the development and growth of American society for the first two hundred years.

In the last three decades or so and particularly in the last ten years, this notion of the common good has largely been supplanted by a belief in the rights of the individual. The right of the individual to pursue personal goals that may even be in conflict with the common good is also being acknowledged. The result is a general loosening up of conventional standards that the individual previously was bound to conform to. For anyone who lived through the turbulence of the sixties with its civil and moral upheaval, this point doesn't need much elaboration.

The practical consequence of public acceptance of the notion of individual fulfillment and individual rights is that there is almost no institution today that can rule by fear. There is almost no institution today that can expect the uncritical loyalty of its members or of the public. There is almost no institution today that can discipline people without repercussion.

Certainly, the American corporation has been

heavily on the receiving end of this change in attitude in recent years. Earlier the corporation had been seen by most Americans as good because it was the mechanism for developing our industrial system, which in turn gave people jobs and transformed capital into profits, which assured further development. It was good for us, and if a few people got chewed up by its relentless growth and its need for strong backs and natural resources, so be it. The common good must be served.

The swing of the pendulum from the common good to the good of the individual is like most pendulum swings. In the recent past it has probably swung too far in this new direction. In the years ahead it will have to right itself somewhat if we are to have a properly balanced society capable of attending to its larger needs as well as of respecting the needs of its individual members. But it would seem that there is little chance that we shall ever return to the days when the common good won every single time over the needs of any individual or group of individuals.

And *there* is the source of conflict for many businesspeople who would really like to ignore this change or to wish it away somehow. It is the reason that so many of them have a siege mentality about their organizations and want to do battle with the government, the consumer groups, and even their own employees. In such organizations communication is reduced to an effort to persuade the rest of the world that the goose will continue laying golden eggs only on its own terms. Therefore, all government regulation is regarded as undue harassment. All consumer protest is seen as unfair complaining from antibusiness interests. All employee unrest is seen as the ingratitude of malcontents.

The problem is that the public at large is in a very different frame of mind from these businesspeople. The notion of serving the common good has generally been set aside (except by institutional leaders) in favor of the radical notion that the individual is important and that his or her needs must be considered in the decision-making process. This notion is radical for the simple reason that for most of this country's history, we have been guided by the principle that the individual might well have to compromise his or her interests if it seemed to promote the general welfare to do so.

This new interest in the rights and needs of the individual certainly adds to the uneasiness people have about large organizations. And yet, ironically, most people in our society are fated to work in and for large organizations for most of their lives. The size and complexity of our society simply demands it.

It is a fascinating problem, and I believe it is part of the reason that the American public has taken a renewed interest in its once placid relationship with its institutions. From all of this has emerged this *third* position on our continuum of business creeds. It is at the extreme opposite end of the classical creed that said business's role toward society should be merely passive and uninvolved. It argues instead that the corporation's power is based on *public* consent.

To put that position into practice, the public has organized itself into various constituencies with which

147

corporate executives must deal. The environmental movement, the consumer movement, trade unions and professional unions and associations, and, most important, the power of the federal and state government—all are serving to enforce the principle that corporate power is subject to public consent. Back we go to the original question. What does this have to do with the problem of corporate communication and corporate credibility?

It is clear that all of this has profound implications for corporate communication. We are, I believe, into the era of relationship. People both inside and outside our various organizations will believe us and trust us on the basis of their relationships with us. This fact immediately alters both the purpose and the style of organizational communication. If society has sour relationships with large organizations, if those organizations are seen as being indifferent to the welfare of their employees, their customers, and their investors, there will be serious repercussions. That should be evident.

The difficult question is how can large corporations establish relationships? How can they cut through their procedures and the demands that come at them from every side, to deal with people as people? In my judgment this is the question that should be preoccupying communications professionals. Not the matter of what kind of publication to solve what kind of organizational problem. Publications and formalized communication programs are too often the stuff that preoccupy us. The truth that all too often goes unspoken and that most of us really know in our heart of hearts is that publications can only provide the scenery and the staging as a backdrop for the real communication that takes place *through relationship.*

It's interesting that the polls all show the same thing—that big business is in trouble with the American public. For example, four out of every ten adult Americans think that big corporations place themselves above the law and can get away with just about anything. More than half believe that big corporations got to be big by manipulating the market in some unfair way, and this particular majority thinks that big corporations should be regulated more tightly.[1]

A large segment of the American public is disappointed, dissatisfied, and dismayed with the everyday performance of American business. This dissatisfaction, I am convinced, comes to a much greater extent from their personal experience as consumers and as employees than it does from what they read in the media. If you are taken for granted, dehumanized, and robbed of your dignity (and sometimes of your livelihood) by a large, impersonal organization, is it any wonder that you do not think highly of large organizations? If you have been had by the various manufacturers of the products you spend your hard-earned money on, is it any wonder that you are a bit disenchanted about their claims of excellence and performance and their often useless warranties?

A recent issue of *U.S. News and World Report* featured an article entitled "Why Business Has a Black Eye." A survey of over 5,000 consumers shows busi-

149

ness is weakest in communicating with the public and its own employees, in demonstrating interest in its customers, in providing value for the money, in dealing with shortages, in controlling pollution, in conserving natural resources, and in being honest in what it says about its products.[2]

There are many people in business and in some of our other institutions who believe that much of the anti-institutionalism we are now experiencing is a product of Watergate and Vietnam. Stanley Marcus, president of Nieman-Marcus, disputes this as a cop-out. He says, "If the reputation of Nieman-Marcus were to begin to slide, I wouldn't ask the local religious leaders if church attendance had fallen off. I wouldn't ask the politicians if voter registration were down. I wouldn't even ask our competitors if their sales were sagging. I'd ask what *we* were doing at Nieman-Marcus to hurt our own reputation." [1]

I said earlier that I believe the magic word is relationship. A clue that I may be right is found in the fact that the same public that feels so negative about big business feels differently about small business. Another recent poll asked Americans to rank their various institutions for honesty, dependability, and integrity. *Small* business was ranked second only to banks—and *ahead* of organized religion. Big business was a distant sixteenth, beating out only advertising agencies, the two political parties, labor leaders, and politicians.[1]

I would suggest that the difference in attitudes toward big business and small business has to do with the key ingredient of relationship. Let me give you a personal example. Where I live, there are two grocery stores where I usually shop. One is part of a large, locally owned chain. The other is a small partnership of four or five men. It is a small store that emphasizes quality and friendly, personal service.

When I go to the branch of the large chain store, I invariably have to wait in line because only three or four of their ten or twelve cash registers are open. After standing in line with my gallon of milk and pound of coffee for seven or eight minutes if I'm lucky, I am moved swiftly by the cashier without even a nod or a mumbled hello, despite a notice next to the time clock demanding that each cashier greet each customer before ringing up the sale. It is strictly a volume operation, and I doubt that any one of the cashiers could pick me out of a police line-up, despite the fact that I'm there perhaps four or five times a week.

At the small store, I never wait in line more than two or three minutes, and the man at the meat counter and the high school age boy who checks me out both call me by name. Every item in that store is a few cents more, but given a choice if both stores are open, I invariably go to the small store and pay the premium. Why? It's totally a matter of relationship. I matter at the small store. At the big one I mean nothing.

The small businessman knows his customer, and his customer knows him. That is one reason why the public is more tolerant of butchers than of meat packers, of bakers than of wheat producers, and of candle makers than of utility companies.

To me the lesson is clear. *We in the big business community must learn how to build and maintain quality relationships. We in the communications profession particularly must learn how to assist our senior managers in all functions in establishing and encouraging both customer and employee relationships.* With consumers, it means being more accessible. It means identifying with their needs and problems. It means talking with them to understand how well or how badly we are serving them. It means making good on all of our promises and not promising anything we can't deliver.

With the employee, it means something pretty basic and simple. It means establishing credibility. It means establishing trust. And it means recognition of the employee's humanity, personal rights, and dignity. In communication terms it requires the manager to be open and honest and not to try to con people. It means honesty in your daily transactions with the people in the work group. And, perhaps most of all, it means recognizing and serving the human needs of your people with some sort of expression of love and concern. Intense listening, a pat on the back, having the guts to say, "I'm sorry"—the possibilities are endless.

In many businesses all of this will mean a very different orientation because the organization has taken on a life and existence of its own and people are preoccupied with serving it. They have forgotten why the business was started in the first place.

It is interesting that it is possible to match particular communication styles of organizations with the business creeds held by their senior managements.

This is obviously an oversimplification, since most managements cannot be easily pigeonholed, but I believe there is a correlation between the business beliefs held by managers and the extent to which they communicate. For example, the classical manager who believes that the market system controls everything and that he has no particular responsibility to anyone except his customers and his shareholders tends to want to communicate very little. If such a person is in a key position of responsibility, you can expect that there will be little meaningful communication with employees or with the public at large.

Basically this person's attitude is that it is no one's affair how the business is run. Such a manager or such a managerial staff would contend that the needs of society are best served if the corporation devotes its full energies to serving its shareholders. The successful operation of the business depends on the consumer's receiving a fair product at a fair cost. Increased sales in turn permit more jobs and a better standard of living. And higher profits mean greater tax revenues. What it boils down to is the notion that the corporation can best serve society by serving itself.

In general, this is the person who is loudest in his denunciation of government interference and government bungling. He simply wants business left alone to serve the common good through its own special interests.

Those who believe in the managerial creed, which argues that the manager's job is to keep all the conflicting and confusing interests in proper balance, very often rely on communication sleight of hand to

153

serve their vision of the organization—for the simple reason that the various and sometimes conflicting interests of employees, shareholders, and customers often require the manager to make decisions that are favorable to one constituency and unfavorable to another. For example, an expensive contract with the bargaining unit may drive a company's cost structure out of line. Management concludes that the shareholders' earnings would be adversely affected, and thus orders a price increase to offset the costs of the contract.

The announcement of the price increase can mean some very difficult customer communication. Or taking this example a step further, management may discover that the new price in a highly competitive market has a disastrous effect on sales. Over a period of time, it may become necessary to reduce overhead in order to live with declining revenue. When this happens, management often turns to a layoff as the solution. In such an instance, once again the problem of communication is extremely delicate.

Because the professional manager often finds himself or herself on the horns of this kind of dilemma, he or she is tempted to produce messages that will be acceptable to all parties. The usual fear is that the truth will not be accepted or that it will make management look incompetent. In the organizational world, appearances are terribly important, so the professional communicator is put to work to produce a skillful, rather than a strictly truthful, statement.

And this is where the verbal sleight of hand comes in. The trouble is that such statements are either unbelievable, and so the audience does not believe them, or they are ignored by the audiences at whom they are directed and who often have enough real information to draw their own conclusions. It is a silly, silly game, but it is played daily by people who believe that their saying that something is true means that everyone will accept it as they've said it.

One of the crosses of all professional communications people in organizations is approval of such statements by senior managers. Countless hours are expended on selecting and polishing words and seeking exactly the right tone and effect. Even the punctuation and capitalization sometimes become an issue between the communicator and a nervous senior or middle manager. It would be funny if the whole thing weren't so painful—and so futile. For the audience will assess the message according to its own experience and perspective regardless of what is said on that piece of paper. Yet those who still believe in word magic persevere, unshaken in their "faith."

It is no accident, though it is certainly ironic, that public relations people have such a poor professional image. They are seen as enemies rather than as facilitators of real communication. Prostitution has ever been prostitution, and I suppose that those who are willing to sell their minds and their pens to the highest bidder deserve the labels they get. The trouble is that bad communication hurts our collective credibility in business whether we are talking about employee communication, public relations, advertising, or public affairs.

My point is that a business leader's beliefs about

155

his or her role in the business profoundly affect both the substance and the style of communication. Those who accept the managerial creed as an explanation of what they are hired to do too often communicate with more of an eye on appearances than on the truth. In the long term, I believe this practice invites disaster.

Just how far this can carry you can be illustrated by a recent experience of mine at a communicators' conference. The speaker was a senior communications official for one of the nation's large steel companies, and his subject was how business might better communicate its message to the federal government and particularly to those regulatory agencies that might be tempted to sponsor restrictive legislation. An interesting subject in a day when more and more businesspeople are feeling the eye of government scrutiny of their daily activities.

But the official's position was appalling. He said that there were essentially four things that any company should do. First, it should centralize all of its communication activities. Second, it should understand and stress constituency relationships. What he meant by that was explained in his third point, which was that the company should help elect certain congressmen and continue to support them for reelection if they supported the company's views. This was a blatant suggestion that his company supporters should remind him of that support when they needed his vote. "That's politics" was his justification for that recommendation, and he added, "You've got to know and help your friends."

His fourth proposal was that the company launch

a campaign with local newspaper editors so that they would write editorials favorable to the company's position. You then clipped out the editorials and sent them on to your friends in Washington as evidence of the popularity and the logic of your position as well as of the "back home" support. And, of course, you should mobilize your employees to write letters when you needed "a public outcry."

The man who was saying all this was a personable and fatherly business executive offering friendly "professional advice" to his peers. And not a single one of them challenged him on the vital matter of the public good. They were too busy taking notes and chuckling conspiratorially.

Doubtless the reason for this reaction is that people in business today often do feel besieged. And it's not a long inductive leap from that feeling to the rationalization that the end justifies the means. That does not, however, make that unsavory doctrine any more palatable than it ever has been.

As I mentioned earlier, the final business position on our imaginary continuum is the consent doctrine, the notion that the corporation derives its franchise from public consent and that if the public is dissatisfied with the corporation's performance, it has a right to reclaim the franchise. The key is corporate performance in serving the ends that are important to the public. In that regard, economist and futurist Carl Madden argues that in the future the public will evaluate corporations by three major criteria: social performance in traditional markets, social performance in the "public needs" market, and social performance in achieving noneconomic values deemed important by society.[3]

Madden goes on to say that the corporation will face a number of significant challenges to its right to exercise its power. Because laissez faire is not trusted to yield social benefit, business power is being curbed and shaped by government and nongovernment groups. Madden predicts a business–government partnership marked by higher standards of conduct and greater public disclosure. He also suggests that corporate managers will no longer be able to take the classic position that their decisions are purely economic. These economic decisions, he argues, will be politicized through the efforts of political action groups, each pursuing its own ends and each arguing for its right to influence business decision making.

The greatest danger Madden sees in all of this is the possibility that economic power will become concentrated in the hands of the government. Today the government employs one out of six U.S. workers and controls about 37 percent of our total spending. Madden's concern, and certainly the concern of vast numbers of business leaders, is what the burden will be on business in the years ahead. Will regulation and government challenges hamper productivity and damage the delicate market system we have put together? The answer to this question depends on how we address the difficult problem of business and society relationships.

One thing does seem to be clear, however, and that is that the traditional self-indulgent attitude of the American corporation must be put behind us. The signals from the American public are that business must be responsive to a variety of public needs and, if necessary, it will be responsive at the direction of government.

This consent doctrine certainly does not presume a passive and silent business organization meekly reacting to every demand made of it. Nor, in my judgment, does it require a quarrelsome and snarling saber-toothed tiger fighting for its very existence.

The proper posture will be an enlightened and ethical leadership of the marketplace and of public opinion. In that regard, Madden holds that public needs could become a big new market for corporate performance. Housing, education, health, transportation, waste management, pollution control—these are only a few of our major needs waiting for business enterprise to address them with the same aggressiveness with which it has invented new brands of deodorant, fast-food outlets, and an infinite variety of pet foods.

Certainly, any corporate management operating with a clear understanding of its responsibility to address public needs will be concerned about effective communication. The very word "consent" implies that you have presented your case and that you have won approval for the course of action you are proposing. In the years ahead the business organization will have to present its own case forcefully and honestly to its employees, to the citizens of the communities with whom it shares the environment and its natural resources, to all of its prospective customers, to its investors, and perhaps most important to both federal and local government.

The notion of government as a relentless adversary will have to be changed. The siege mentality of many business leaders will also have to go. In its place must come the understanding that the public has the right to try to influence the corporation through the political process as well as in the marketplace. With this must come the acknowledged and accompanying right of business to play an active role in influencing the political values and choices of the community and to participate actively in the process of setting economic and social goals for the country.

The one caveat is that this process must be carried on *honestly* and *openly*. I don't mind my colleague from the steel company trying to influence the vote of his congressman in a way that is favorable to his company's positions as long as he does it at an open hearing or in other open forums. I do object to his doing it in the back of the company plane on the way to Aruba or in the congressman's campaign office a few weeks before election.

There's a world of difference between these two methods, and we in business had better understand that difference if we are to cope successfully with the emerging public demands that will shape our actions in the years ahead.

CHAPTER VII

But Will They Be Happy and Productive?

THE trouble with most organizational communication is its thin philosophical foundation. Most people in the business world still believe that the main reason you communicate with people at work is to make them happy and productive. And it drives them crazy when people who are well informed are not happier and more productive as a result of intense communication efforts.

The reason can be found in both the history and nature of work. Psychologist Erich Fromm tells us that work is man's liberator from nature. In the process of changing and molding nature, the individual changes and molds himself or herself. The more his work develops, the more his individuality develops. That fact is most obvious in true craftsmanship. The craftsman loves his craft. It is part of himself and is an expression of who and what he is. There is no separation of work and play or work and culture.[1]

Before industrialization, people worked to meet their physical and material needs in a struggle that filled most of their waking hours. This struggle was real and it was very much a part of their existence. They did not have far to search for the meaning of their lives. They were providers for themselves and for others, and the process of providing was their work.

With the collapse of the rural, subsistence economy or, more accurately, with the rise of modern industrialization, the nature of work changed fundamentally. For the vast majority of people who had only their physical energy to sell, work became, in a sense, "forced" labor. Workers in the eighteenth and nineteenth centuries who had to work 16-hour days to keep from starving did so because they had little choice but to sell their labor to those who had the means to capitalize on it. As it became possible to amass material wealth by work, work became more and more a pure *means* to achieving the aim of success and wealth, however that success or wealth might be defined.

In more recent times, as technology has developed and as the drive to make bigger and better things became an aim in itself, work has become increasingly separate from the worker. Automation and large, impersonal organizations have tended to make workers part of the *apparatus* of production and to compartmentalize their lives. The result has been to alienate people from their work.

Increasing attention has been paid in recent years to the psychology of the worker and to his attitude toward his work. Fromm says that the very formulation of this notion of "the human problem of industry" is indicative of the underlying attitude of the research. In his view what should be discussed is people's industrial problem rather than industry's people problem.[1] The difference is enormous.

Most of the work in industrial psychology has been directed at the question of how worker productivity can be increased and how friction of workers with one another and with the organization can be reduced. Fromm observes that in the name of human relations, the worker is treated with all the devices that suit a completely alienated person. Even happiness and "human values" are supported in the interests of efficiency and productivity. The hope is that happier people will produce more. Thus human values are advocated not in their own name and for their own sake, but as a means of *using* people.[1]

We have become curiously indifferent to this situation, and most people in business rarely give it a thought. Unhappily, there is a long-standing tradition in employee communication that such is the essence of our work. We should communicate with people so that they will not be distracted by misinformation and rumors, so that they will have "high

163

morale" and be loyal to the organization, and so that they will be motivated toward greater productivity.

To prove to you that I did not invent that explanation, let me quote some findings of a recent communication survey prepared by *The Corporate Communications Report.*[2] The survey was sent to the presidents of the Fortune 1000 companies and 300 "other" major companies. The sponsor of the survey, Corpcom Services, offered seven traditional employee communication tasks (which are revealing in themselves) and asked the respondents to choose the three they considered most important and to rate them first, second, and third. The total number of mentions for each item was computed and ranked. The results are as shown in Table 2.

Fromm's observation that these kinds of devices represent a prescription for dealing with an alienated person is not far from the mark. Except for the second and seventh items, each one of these things is an attempt to foster behavior or qualities that should be second nature to a satisfied worker. They are also the kind of measures that you would expect to see recommended as a prescription for dealing with depersonalization.

What troubles me about this list is that too many communications professionals accept these kinds of goals uncritically and are willing to commit themselves to their achievement. Moreover, the means they select to accomplish them involve printed matter almost exclusively. And it is not uncommon for *one* editor with only *one* newspaper or *one* magazine to promise to work for the attainment of such complex goals as fostering loyalty and reducing turnover.

TABLE 2. Corpcom survey of traditional employee communication tasks.

Rank	Item	Percentage who selected item
1	To build morale and foster employee loyalty to the company.	90
2	To keep employees informed and avoid misinformation and rumors.	88.9
3	To motivate employees toward greater productivity.	77.8
4	To create an employee constituency that will support the company with legislators and on other public fronts.	50.8
5	To reduce employee turnover.	50.0
6	To help avoid strikes and other labor unrest.	41.3
7	To encourage employees to invest in the company.	29.4

Source: "Employee Communications Survey 1975," a survey conducted by *The Corporate Communications Report,* January 1976, pp. 3–4.

Even where the communications repertoire goes beyond the simple house organ, that would be an impossible task. I have to believe that no intelligent management that reflects on the problems of human communication and these proposed solutions for more than five or ten minutes really believes that anything significant will happen. Management generally finances such ventures on the misguided notion that they can't really hurt anything, and they just might help a little bit. The fact of the matter is that they can hurt a lot. Giving a band-aid to a person who is hemorrhaging before your very eyes may constitute legitimate first aid, but if that's all your treatment consists of, it's cruel and inhuman.

Today most organizations go well beyond the band-aid if they have any concern for effective communication with their people. It is not too unusual in these times to find competent professional staffs, in our large companies particularly, producing slick management newsletters, artful television programs on video tape or video cassettes, elaborate telephone message systems, and a whole host of other programs in addition to the employee newspaper or magazine.

The trouble is that a good share of what is done is still addressed to achieving the seven traditional goals listed above (or variations thereof). And therein lies the problem because you can't build employee loyalty at the other end of a television set any better than you can at the other end of a newspaper. Employee loyalty is a human problem to be resolved by human beings face to face, day after day.

Half recognizing that, communications people tend to turn inward on their media and on the perfection of their technical skills in the pitiful belief that if only they could do a better job, the communication problems would be solved. For their part, senior managements console themselves with the tangible products their communications people produce and tacitly agree not to ask any embarrassing questions about the overall impact on the problem of alienated and disapproving workers.

Communication consultant Mike Emanuel summed up the situation in a comment in a magazine interview on the state of the art in employee communication:

You would think . . . that smart businessmen, having
been involved in a long-term venture costing hundreds
of millions of dollars literally in direct expenditure, and
perhaps twice that much in contributed time and everything else, would have all this buttoned down. Right?
Who you're talking to, what they know and don't know,
what moves them and what doesn't. Let me tell you
something . . . it doesn't exist. It's appalling.[3]

In too many cases the communications professionals themselves are also confused about their roles
and their responsibilities. They don't know whether
they are journalists, the voice of management, rep-
resentatives of the employee public, or just hired
guns. The result is that they do their jobs as well as
they can in light of their understanding of those jobs.
Often they do well; sometimes they do badly.

The solution, I believe, is rather simple. Step one
is for the communications professional to decide who
he or she is and what the job is. For anyone not directly connected with this discipline, that step may
appear ridiculously obvious. But there is very real
confusion over both objectives and responsibilities. In
my years in this business, I've observed three dis-
tinctly different positions on this subject.

Perhaps the most prevalent position is the "I-
just-work-here" attitude. In some organizations that
may be a very realistic and even intelligent response
to the job and the way it's structured. In others it may
reflect the communicator's own short-sightedness or
lack of imagination. In practically every instance it is
the lament of an editor or a manager who believes
that his or her own management is not really interested in communicating with its employees.

Once the professional communicator arrives at

that conclusion, he or she simply goes through the motions. Because they have professional pride in most instances, their solution generally is to become expert technicians. Which I believe explains why there is so much emphasis on technique in the professional organizations to which communications people belong. Endless hours at meetings and in professional publications are spent on writing and photographic skills and other questions of "how to do it better." The *why* of what we are doing is seldom even mentioned.

I believe that the reason for this is that most people in this business believe they have little or no control over their work. Their attitude is that they must wait to be told, and then they must have permission for each and every word they produce on management's behalf. If they don't have control over their work, they do have control over the media they use. Thus the emphasis on the media, which they can control, and the disregard of the message, which they can't control. I overstate to make my point, but I don't overstate by much.

Reacting to this situation, many of my colleagues argue that the responsibility of the editor or communications manager is to stand up to his or her own management and to become the corporate hair shirt. Their vision of this role is that the communicator should represent the needs and interests of his or her audience and should argue forcefully their right to know. This is a romantic view of the problem that has some appeal, especially to people who see themselves as refugees from journalism and who, worse yet, believe they have "sold out" to business.

While it may be the stuff of good movie or TV plots, it is a very unrealistic view of the role of communicators and of what they can and should do. Nobody likes hair shirts, and there's a good chance that they will be removed at the first opportunity.

There is a third possibility that has great merit. It is for professional communicators to see themselves as *facilitators of change.* To be such a facilitator, you must first understand what is happening to all of our modern institutions in terms of the value changes they must deal with and in terms of the attitudes of the workforce. Once you understand those changes and accept them as real directions that our society is at least exploring, you are then in a position to ask the crucial question of what, if anything, these changes mean to the short- and long-term future of your own organization.

This question is one that people in every organization are struggling with if they are trying to come to grips with the future course of that organization. What do such changes mean in the marketplace? What do they mean in the larger society? What effect will they have on the structure and operation of the organization, not to mention its very mission? What will they do to the people who make the organization run?

When you identify the people who are wrestling with these questions in your own company, I recommend that you get to know them (whatever their titles and specialties) and their work. That applies whether you are a professional communicator or any other kind of specialist or senior manager. The professional communicator can easily forge an alliance with such people and can assist them in preparing the organization's people for the likely changes they will need to understand and respond to.

Perhaps most important, he or she can help employees understand the *meaning* of their lives in the work place. I have to believe that the traditional employee communication goals of encouraging loyalty and greater productivity would be much better served *if* people truly understood the meaning of their lives and *if* from that meaning they were able to foster a personal sense of hope for the future. People who do not understand change tend to lose hope. That loss normally means further alienation from work and with it greater absenteeism, less trust and therefore less loyalty, less sense of purpose and therefore less productivity.

The role of facilitator will not solve all of the problems of the professional communicator or the organization, but it will make communication with employees one of the most valuable and most honorable of the communication specialties because it will be helping to establish the connection between people's humanity and their work lives. Beginning from that orientation, communicators will perform their jobs in very different ways. For one thing they will never allow themselves to become narrow technicians.

The role of facilitating change will fall not to technicians, but to people who are capable of conceptual thinking. If you are going to be successful first in persuading corporate management that it will have to communicate the directions and the long-range objectives of the business and then in actually carrying on that kind of communication, you will have to be able to articulate the why and the how of such communication. Persuading senior management that this is what employee communication is really about usually is not an easy task. In general, management's orientation is toward more tangible, concrete kinds of communication efforts, which probably explains why employee communication typically is restricted to newspapers, magazines, and the like.

The professional communicator who sees himself or herself in the role of facilitator must be prepared for a certain amount of resistance and misunderstanding. Ian Wilson of General Electric's business environment research staff has summed up the problem: "We have institutionalized change in our society without changing our institutions. It is as if we had believed that all the physical attributes of our society could be in flux without there being any fundamental change in our value systems or our social organization. Such a belief is absurd; yet only now are we coming to realize it." [4]

What the professional communicator must be prepared to do is to persuade his or her own management that the organization must understand the turmoil inside and outside its walls and then share that understanding with the employees so that they can comprehend and adapt. Otherwise, the large organization risks even greater employee alienation as it tries to pretend that it can create an internal environment that is insulated from the changes in the larger society. I can't imagine a less promising employee communication strategy than preaching to people on the values of profit, productivity, loyalty, and the threat of government regulation. These are still significant organizational issues, but sermons stated in traditional corporate terms are not likely to connect with the values and experience of the audience.

Younger employees in particular are inclined to be indifferent to the company's profit position because they see little connection between it and their personal well-being. They regard productivity as a code word that means the boss wants them to work harder and look busier. Loyalty to organizations is a foreign concept to them because they have grown up to distrust organizations and to see mobility and job change as the norm. And finally they tend to believe that big business would probably benefit from a little intelligent regulation. Mere sermons won't have much effect on these attitudes and beliefs.

The important question is: What will have an effect on these attitudes and beliefs? The best answer I know of is *proactive communication,* which is a fancy way of saying that we must anticipate problems and opportunities and talk about them in terms that mean something to both our internal and external audiences.

To this end it is important for corporate planners to develop a good early warning system. Not every "blip" on the radar screen will continue on its apparent course, and some "blips" may be transient phenomena. Sorting out which of today's events will have lasting impact on us and which will flash across the sky like a falling star is not easy, but it certainly is important. There is risk of error in this sort of anticipation, but there is merit in being forewarned even if some of the predicted changes don't occur.

So it's important for both the senior manager and the communications professional to become students of their own organization's needs and problems and students of changing attitudes and expectations. When they reach agreement that a given change or trend is real and that it is likely to affect the organization in some significant way, they must together do two things. They must factor the new trend into the organization's objectives, and they must develop a clear-cut rationale for the change in question.

It is no longer enough for any manager to say, "So be it." The rationale that is communicated to employees (and it must be communicated if there is any hope of employee understanding and commitment) must seek to induce change by stressing the *opportunities* that change can realize as well as the *threats* it may try to head off.

Ian Wilson says that the rationale should emphasize the marketing opportunities that the change represents for the organization; that it should focus on productivity opportunities in persuading people that their talents can and will be directed at the solution of an interesting and challenging organizational problem; and that it should take advantage of the organization's resolve to take action in anticipation of social needs and concerns rather than be led by the nose by an irate consumer or public.[5]

Three things are implicit in this kind of communication. One is top management's commitment to move the organization in these carefully planned directions along with the resolve to communicate why and how. The second is the need for a comprehensive organizational plan to achieve this change and to institutionalize it on a systematic and sustained basis. And the third is the need for specific goals and objectives so that such change is orderly and effective. None of this is particularly new in a well-managed organization, but it is of the essence of successful organizational change.[6]

Working in this way the communicator gets out of one of the traditional binds of the profession. He or she stops *reacting* to every piece of organization "news" and begins to *propagandize* intelligently for needed change. There is a world of difference in those two modes. In the first the communicator is the frustrated and unappreciated reporter unwittingly threatening his or her own management by wanting to report the problems and the setbacks to company plans. In the second he or she is the trusted ally helping to bring about necessary changes in the culture of the organization.

Even more significant, the communicator is working from a carefully developed communication plan that is driven by the need to communicate certain truths about the organization's future and its well-being. That plan gives his efforts a sense of purpose and direction that he can never achieve when he is merely reacting to company events and reporting them in chaotic and unconnected pieces.

Does this mean that the communicator will never report anything but good news? Absolutely not. It means that the setbacks and the failures are reported within a framework that gives them increased significance to the audience. In the role I am outlining here for the professional communicator and for organizational management in general, effective planning is critical. It is also imperative for both management and communicators to recognize the very real limitations of formal media and the essential relationship of these media to interpersonal communication.

Finally, in this role, the communicator's most important task is to work to understand the complex culture of his or her organization and to work within that culture for constructive change. From that understanding comes what I regard as the real mission of communication with employees—helping people to comprehend their work lives and to find within that critical part of their lives meaning, hope, and satisfaction.

Let's reduce all of this to a specific example by looking at our imaginary company in Chapter 1, Acme Chemical Company. If you recall, Acme is a rather reactionary organization attuned to attitudes and values of the past. Security, conformity, and paternalism are its most noticeable organizational characteristics. But there is trouble brewing in the form of people's attitudes toward the way they are being managed.

In sum, Acme people report that the prevailing management style is autocratic and restrictive. People are encouraged not to be innovative and not to make

175

waves, and when something goes wrong, the boss looks to find out who is to blame and reprimands that person openly. The whole atmosphere is reminiscent of a nineteenth-century organization with its emphasis on paternalism and control.

But a new element is being introduced in the form of Japanese competition in the marketplace. The former stranglehold that Acme held on the market has been broken, with the result that both sales and earnings are eroding. For Acme it is a new experience.

Acme president Fred Eaton is acutely aware that something must be done to change the generally complacent attitudes of the employees. He is a long-term Acme employee himself, having joined the company fresh out of college some 35 years earlier. Unlike most of the senior staff, Eaton is a progressive manager who has never been afraid of change. Since taking over the presidency 18 months ago, he has tried conscientiously to move his own candidates into the key management positions. This has been a very difficult task since it is generally understood at Acme that senior people hold their positions until retirement. Through some very careful persuasion and a generous retirement settlement, he has managed to put out to pasture some of the more hidebound Acme senior people.

His new vice president of corporate communication is Ted Forester, a man Eaton recruited for the specific purpose of updating Acme communication, with special emphasis on the employee audience. Eaton is anxious to do three things. First, he wants to reverse the traditional close-to-the-vest communication posture at Acme so that people will understand the company's problems and priorities. (He is especially interested in persuading Acme managers to do a better job of communicating with their own people.) Second, he wants to educate people about the competitive threats to the Acme market position, and he wants to give them a sense of greater urgency about meeting and besting this competition. And, finally, he believes that Acme will have to change its internal culture considerably to cope with the pressures and the demands of the next couple of decades. This last need has him particularly concerned because he does not want to wrench the company suddenly from its paternalistic tradition, for fear that the trauma would be too severe for Acme people. Because of the impact of competition, he does, however, want to educate the people to the need to change the way Acme has operated.

The entire Acme communication "program" is a weekly publication begun in 1935 and published continuously since that time. *The Acme Recorder* has always been dedicated to employee hobbies, recognition of unusual employee accomplishments, and announcements of coming events of the employee recreation association. Its readers have valued it chiefly for its outstanding classified ads section. This feature occupies at least one and sometimes two of the issue's eight pages every week, so that employees will be able to buy and sell one another's cast-offs or moonlighting services. The front page of every issue is dedicated to reporting on new products and to recogniz-

177

ing the work achievements of Acme people. The "news" is rarely, if ever, new.

Forester has spent his first six months at Acme studying the lay of the land. He has read and reread every available report and survey on employee attitudes at Acme. At every opportunity he has carefully observed Eaton and his entire staff. He has interviewed each of Eaton's senior staff people to assess their opinions about the business and its future opportunities and problems. He has analyzed in detail both this year's operating plan and the long-range business plan.

In his efforts to get to know the members of Eaton's senior staff, Forester has built the best working relationship with the vice president of personnel and with one of his direct reports, the manager of human resources planning and training, Roberta Bogart. Bogart is a gold mine of information about Acme people problems. She knows who the effective and ineffective managers are. She knows which Acme plants have what kind of labor relations problems, and she understands the Acme corporate culture thoroughly.

The editor of *The Acme Recorder* is John English, an ex-newspaper reporter who has been publishing the *Recorder* for the last 23 years. English is a reasonably competent technician who many years earlier happily accepted the fact that the *Recorder* was to be just another house organ. In keeping with Acme's practice of liberal hiring, the *Recorder* has four full-time staff people. The newspaper is their sole job and has been for some years.

Once Forester understands the problems he's up against, he puts together an employee communication plan that will strive to accomplish the three major communication goals that Eaton has told him are important to the company's future success. His first staff action three months ago was to replace English as editor with a bright young woman who is a very strong writer and a particularly good interviewer and feature writer.

Next he hired a man who could write and produce a management newsletter and who could also counsel the senior staff on its own communication problems, as necessary.

Beginning with the management newsletter and a revamped version of *The Acme Recorder,* Forester is building some core communication programs that will serve Acme needs in the years ahead. His first priority has been the establishment by him and his staff of message goals, on which every program, project, or story must be based. The design of the *Recorder* has been changed completely, and gone are the classified ads, gone are the hobby stories, and gone are the postage-stamp-size pictures of retirees and anniversary celebrants.

Forester's logic is that in a company of 20,000 people, such pictures are irrelevant. The ads were a particularly emotional issue with the *Recorder*'s staff since they believed this device attracted readers they might not get otherwise. Forester's reaction was that they were ducking their editorial responsibility to produce a publication people would want to read. They reluctantly agreed to the change, and despite the dire predictions, only two or three complaints have been received about discontinuing the ad service.

The service anniversaries and the retirements have been handled by the simple device of posting the picture of the person being honored on a bulletin board in his or her work area. A special standardized mount has been designed for this purpose according to the number of years of service. The people who really care about such things—namely the subjects and their co-workers—are perfectly satisfied with this solution. Most important, valuable space has been freed in the *Recorder* for the subjects that need to be communicated in some depth.

Forester and his editor are running stories about Acme people dealing with some of the difficult issues now facing the company. They are lively, well-written, and real, and Acme people who read the publication will very quickly be able to understand the nature of the problems the company is facing. Most of the editorial emphasis is on the basic question: What does all of this mean to *you* as an employee? How does it affect *your* career and *your* future?

These changes have not been easy to make. Even Eaton himself was uneasy in the beginning about this approach. When Forester interviewed Eaton for the first issue of the revamped *Recorder,* he asked him a series of very tough questions about the business and elicited some equally tough answers. Eaton circulated the interview copy for review by his senior staff and received a number of negative reactions from the more conservative members. In fact, of his six direct reports, four were against publishing the interview because it was "too frank." Forester was insistent that the first step in any communication effort was a frank discussion of the problems with Acme employees. His position prevailed, and Eaton agreed, with some apprehension, to the publication of the interview.

Overall reaction to the interview and to the first issue was very positive as Acme people finally began to see the dimensions of the business problems they were up against. Forester's next step was to get the management newsletter up and running. Its circulation is restricted to Acme managers, an audience of roughly 1500 people. In interviews and in signed articles, Forester is helping Acme managers to develop an understanding of the important issues at Acme and within the business community in general, as well as giving them tips on how to develop their managerial skills. Much of the emphasis is on the manager's human relations skills and his or her responsibility to manage Acme people effectively.

One very important function of the newsletter is as an extension of the training function. The lessons taught in Acme training seminars often become material for the newsletter and its readers.

Forester has two brand-new programs on the drawing board. One is an employee upward communication program called *Why?* This involves easy-to-use forms that will be posted in heavily traveled company locations such as corridors and cafeterias. Acme employees will be able to use the *Why?* forms to get written answers to their questions and concerns about any and all company issues. The *Why?* letters are passed along anonymously to Acme management for written answers, only one of which Forester's staff is authorized to relay to the particular employee's home address. Forester expects that the program will be a crude measure of what is on employees' minds; he also believes that such a program can be an effective safety valve for people who are frustrated by their attempts to get information from their own managers.

The second program he has been examining and is about to recommend is something he calls *Acme Now*. It is a publication posted on specially reserved sections of company bulletin boards—immediately before public announcements are to be made. The intent is to get information to Acme people *before* they read it or hear it in the public media.

Forester's pet communication project at this time is an employee communication meeting that Eaton held within the last month for some forty randomly selected Acme people. It was a no-holds-barred session that encouraged both presubmitted questions in writing and frank, spontaneous questions from the audience. Although there was some initial shadow boxing and reticence, Eaton was pleasantly surprised to discover that Acme people were not afraid to ask him tough questions and to pursue the answers and their concerns. Eaton himself learned so much and was given such high marks by his audience that he has insisted that his own managers run the same kinds of communication meetings with their own people.

The result of all these efforts has been to quickly and efficiently open up communication channels with

Acme people. They are not all satisfied or happy with what they are hearing, but at least they are being treated like responsible adults with legitimate interests in what is happening to the company, both inside and outside.

This quick summary of Forester's initial efforts makes it sound easy. In fact, he had to work hard to persuade Eaton and his reports that such programs were in the best interests of Acme and Acme people. He was very careful not to make any rash promises about improved morale or increased productivity or other things he knew could not be affected much by mere printer's ink. Instead, he said only that he was trying to provide Acme people with a better understanding of the business and of their own stake in that business.

So far the task has been eased somewhat by the fact that Acme management could see the relationship between the programs he was developing and the present and future problems and plans of the company. They weren't yet convinced that Acme people really needed to be informed about such things, but at least they could see that Forester was not trying to work at cross-purposes to them or to embarrass them.

Privately, Forester believes that it will be a good five years before he is able to have much impact on the Acme corporate culture. He believes it will be that long before Acme middle managers really begin to communicate freely with their own people. In the interim he is interested in producing programs that foster this sort of communication by first talking about the issues and then by using the example of the communication behavior of Acme senior managers. If senior managers run effective communication meetings with their people and if they demonstrate their willingness to talk frankly about the tough issues, he reasons that their managers will do the same thing with their people. Progress is slow, but he already sees indications that this strategy will pay off.

A half dozen simple principles underlie Forester's current work and his plans for the future. At Acme or any other large organization, whether it be a corporation, a university, or a government body, the same basic principles apply. Essentially, they are:

- Effective employee communication must be tailored to the particular needs of the organization.
- It must be proactive, discussing the present and future problems and priorities of the organization and educating people to understand their implications.
- It must be absolutely truthful in stating company plans and positions, which must then be consistent with company actions.
- It must address the *real* concerns of all the people in the organization in terms they can understand. It cannot be aimed at vague issues like productivity and the virtues of the free enterprise system.
- The inherent limitations of formalized communication must be understood by everyone in the organization. Such communication can only be a stage for the real day-to-day interactions of the

people on that stage. It is important, but it cannot be confused with those human interactions.

- And, finally, formalized communication won't motivate anyone. It won't make anyone more productive. It won't increase their loyalty. And it won't make them one damn bit happier.

CHAPTER VIII

Affirmations

THE concern that should nag at any author who tries to describe the truth of contemporary work and contemporary organizations is tunnel vision. In *De-Managing America,* an intriguing book in praise of our collective tendency to do the right and sensible thing despite what the author sees as stupefying mismanagement by our institutional leaders, Richard Cornuelle accuses the American press of being "one-eyed." He says:

> The superstition that America works because the front office manages it is reinforced every day by what we read in the papers. The American press is a front-office press. . . . The more remote and authoritarian an institution, the more likely the press is to report its activities exhaustively. As a result, we are strangers to our own society.[1]

186

Cornuelle's point very simply is that America works in spite of the front office. Because people are intelligent and resourceful, they simply do what they have to do to make their lives livable. It's an interesting and in some ways a very attractive thesis he presents.

But it's also dangerously romantic. Our institutions don't work that well. They are clumsy and bureaucratic. They tend to dehumanize people. So the hell with them. Let us turn our backs on them and simply do the wise and virtuous thing. It's so simple.

My own experience and observation, however, lead me to a different set of conclusions. I see some of the same idiocy that Cornuelle catalogs so delightfully in his attack on the elitist pretensions of American institutional management, but I can't accept the notion that by ourselves and without formal leadership, we will move to correct the inequities and the injustices of authoritarian management.

Because my experience has been totally within organizations, I may be guilty of tunnel vision in believing that we can and must work to make the organization experience more human. But I don't think that it is tunnel vision, for the simple reason that the size and complexity of our society requires that we mobilize large numbers of people to do our work efficiently. The individual cannot really do for himself all the things that are necessary to his well-being in a specialized and urbanized environment.

However, I certainly do not believe that it is inevitable or necessary for such organizations to dehumanize people and to rob them of their dignity.

187

The key to all of this is our *individual* behavior within our various organizations. It is easy for us to allow that to sink to the level of the least common denominator and to be tolerant of all sorts of human abuse in the name of "efficiency" and "results."

I believe that this is why corporate America is in trouble today. As one observer stated in a recent AMA Survey Report:

> [I] wonder whether today's businessmen understand that they are on trial before the American public. . . . [Unless they] provide an environment of stable employment, produce high-quality products and services at reasonable prices, and lead, not follow, the government in improving living conditions for the disadvantaged, the future for business is not as bright as it might otherwise be.[2]

It is a tricky business to make large organizations responsive to high moral standards. By definition, they do not "think" or "agonize" over moral questions. Their behavior is simply the product of the decisions and actions of the people who lead them. If those people behave according to a commonly understood and accepted code, the organization will also behave according to that code. Similarly, the absence of that code will be evident in the organization's policies and actions. In brief, corporations will be as moral and conscientious as their people.

And therein lies a serious and an inescapable truth for all of us who are part of corporate America. The difficulty is that in our headlong rush toward new values to replace many of the old that we have rejected, we have largely ignored the problem of a personal morality and more specifically of a carefully developed sense of how we can and should relate to other people. The proposition that we should care about other people, be sensitive to their needs, and be concerned with how we communicate with them is not popular or well received in most organizations. The unspoken question is: Why? What will it do for *me*? What will it do for the more efficient accomplishment of work goals? Aside from the need to cooperate with other people in doing the work, why should *I* worry about such matters?

There is, in fact, a feeling that concerns of this sort may get in the way of getting the job done. There is the unmistakable, though usually unspoken, view in many institutional organizations that nice guys finish last. The way to success is to be combative and aggressive, and not trust or care about others. Such attitudes normally lead to an environment that is hostile and even brutal. It is an environment that most of us, if we reflect on it, personally despise.

Cornuelle argues that this environment is the product of a series of stupid superstitions that we cling to in contradiction of our common experience. These then become the justification for oppressive measures in and by our various institutions. Among the more commonplace of these superstitions are:

Women are empty-headed, hysterical, and unreliable.

Schoolchildren are lazy and mischievous and resist learning ferociously.

Adolescents are irresponsible, unfit for serious responsibility.

189

Employees are lazy, dishonest, and rebellious.
People in general are larcenous, insensitive to the needs of others, hopelessly narcissistic.
Businessmen are greedy, crooked, base, and unscrupulous.
Consumers are ignorant and gullible.[3]

The trouble with such superstitions—aside from the obvious fact that they are superstitions—is that they have a very strong effect on our behavior. In acting them out, we oppress one another and make of ourselves and each other less than we could be.

I have no glib answers for changing all of this overnight. If there is an answer, it is to be found in our private views of human nature and our willingness to try to impose those views on the various segments of our lives, including the work place. What I am talking about, finally, is nothing less than acting in love toward other people.

For the hard-headed business person who responds only to the fluctuations in the bottom line, such behavior may be close to unthinkable in the work place. And yet that is what all of us really want for *ourselves*. We want to be valued, to be recognized, and to be treated fairly. Giving this to someone else, however, is a different matter.

A friend of mine who is also the spiritual director of a college seminary once told me that it made no sense for anyone to act in love toward another person. Taken at face value, such behavior is preposterous in the sort of organized, urbanized environment in which we live. Only a fool, he pointed out, would love someone who was capable of doing him injury. Only a fool would forgive when he was injured. Only a fool would lead his life in service of the needs of others. As objective facts, these things made no sense. Not only that, such behavior could not be sustained by any individual.

Those in organizations who believe that human values and humane treatment of people are impractical generally justify their beliefs with this kind of "practical" logic. My friend, however, did not stop at that simple roadblock.

If, on the other hand, he reminded me, you have faith, that faith in turn will lead to hope. Without faith in something or someone, there is no hope. That's practically axiomatic. To be hopeful, you must have some basis for that hope. That basis is the source of your hope. For him it was faith in the love and goodness of God. For others it may be the same thing or something different, such as faith in the essential worth of people. Whatever the source of that faith, it is necessary to sustain it and nurture it if one is to be a hopeful person.

This wise priest had concluded long ago that if one truly had faith, one would also have hope, and hopeful persons almost invariably are ministering to their fellow humans. Their lives and their view of those lives offer them little choice. They may waver from time to time. They may occasionally become very discouraged with the whole business, but ultimately they continue ministering. The alternative to hope and to this kind of behavior, my friend has reminded me many times since then, is cynicism. And in his words, "Whom does cynicism really hurt but the cynic?" Again in his words, "It burns your guts out."

I've never forgotten this discussion and my friend's insights. St. Paul said it a little differently: "Meanwhile these three remain: faith, hope, and love; and the greatest of these is love." In my own life in the organization, I have found this to be the most workable formula for both understanding it and succeeding in it.

It or some variation of it is also the justification for treating people decently inside and outside the organization. And it is the real justification for taking the time and energy to communicate fully and truthfully.

Having said that, I recognize that there are still many questions to be addressed about the future of our organizations and their believability in the contemporary world. Many of these questions arise from the generally self-indulgent attitudes of large organizations. The economic power that organizations can wield too often has led them to arrogance and indifference to the public good.

Corporate communicators can produce tons of slick and expensive brochures and hand-outs proclaiming their good intentions, but the history of our organizations in pursuing their own parochial interests, sometimes in outright disregard of the public interest, cannot be easily forgotten. Nor can the recent and sad chapter detailing the number and extent of corporate bribes, campaign contributions, and kickbacks be easily erased.

The hypocrisy of those who rail against government regulation and laud the free enterprise system at the same time that they privately lobby for public subsidies also causes a serious credibility problem. Cornuelle says of this phenomenon, "Businessmen do not, on the whole, believe in free enterprise. They are fervid supporters of the comfortable half of the free enterprise ideal, the part which says business should be free of regulation. But I have never met a businessman who liked competition and who would not evade its discipline if he possibly could." [4]

The feelings of persecution that many business leaders share tend to encourage self-indulgence and to reinforce the public view of businesspeople as soreheads. Geoffrey Barraclough, in his AMA Survey Report entitled *Management in a Changing Economy,* catalogs some of the resentments expressed by the business respondents to his survey:

> Businessmen evidently feel strongly that they are misunderstood, distrusted, and subjected to unfair restraints, and that most of their problems spring from interference and misinformation. Business, they complain, has become a "dirty word"—and profit an even dirtier word. . . .
>
> There is no doubt about the genuineness—and often, indeed, the vehemence—of these resentments. At a rough estimate, at least three-quarters of the respondents felt they were getting a raw deal. The question, of course, is whether resentment is a sound basis for rational judgment. For my part, I find the attitude of the majority of the respondents somewhat disquieting. After all, for business itself, the important thing is not to bemoan the passing of old (probably idealized) values, or to fulminate against the federal government, but to adapt to the environment in which it lives and works. On any

193

> long-term view, this is where its interest lies. The obvious
> danger here is the possibility that shifting responsibility
> onto the shoulders of a scapegoat may stand in the way
> of a necessary process of self-examination and reap-
> praisal.[5]

The Barraclough survey raises two or three other key questions that will affect the ways in which business is perceived in the years ahead by both its employee public and the public at large. All of these directly or indirectly get at the issue of whether the free market system will continue in its present form or whether it will be drastically altered. Specifically, those who responded to the survey were of the opinion that "even in the best of circumstances, the economy is running into a long-term period of slow growth."

In the face of that slow growth, the majority recommended conservative business action almost across the board: conserve assets, cut costs, remain as liquid as possible, reduce capital investment, seek less growth, and avoid risk taking to the greatest extent possible. When respondents were asked to consider a major technological breakthrough that would be good for the economy, the most common responses had to do with energy sources, transportation, conservation of natural resources, pollution control, preservation of the environment, and population.

In this regard, Barraclough notes a significant dichotomy in the attitudes of management. While most managers acknowledge the responsibility of business to respond to the needs of society, they seem to be drawing in their own horns, retrenching, and generally avoiding the challenges that we face as a society.

Barraclough sees in this a threat to the very free market system these business leaders claim they want to preserve. In his words, "And yet this is the question on which the future of business—and perhaps of free enterprise—turns. If it [business] takes up the challenges constructively and shows that it can deliver the goods people want, its future is assured." And then in a foreboding voice, he adds, "But what if it does not?" [6]

The prediction emerges from the survey report that the free market system will continue to evolve as it has for more than the last thirty years into a partnership between business and government. Many of the survey respondents regretted that probability, but felt that it was inevitable in the face of the immense complexity of our industrial society. Such a conclusion seems especially plausible if government has to invest heavily in basic industries such as energy and transportation, which is what the majority of respondents advocated.

Barraclough asserts that most of us know that the "mixed economy" has come to stay. "The important thing to realize at this stage," he says, "is that it *is* a *mixed* economy . . . in which private enterprise has a definite part to play." [7] The caveat he offers is that the mixed approach can be used to benefit everyone *only* if both sides are prepared to work together with good will.

Whether or not this will happen is a crucial question that is difficult to answer at this point in our history. Until now the two potential bedfellows have barely been friends, much less partners. It is clear that each has got to spend considerable time and effort trying to understand the other's problems and point of view. It is also clear that the stereotypes each one holds of the other must be abandoned.

Not the least of these tasks will be the understanding of one another's strengths and weaknesses. Barraclough defines this issue nicely:

> There are undoubtedly areas in which private enterprise does better than a controlled economy; one of them is providing the consumer with a wide variety of goods at competitive prices. There are also areas in which it does not do so well; one certainly . . . is attention to social needs and the preservation of the environment, in which matter the business community has thus far shown an unfortunate insensitivity.[7]

Aside from the questions of who should do what, there is the issue of what the doing will do to us as a free society. The specter of bureaucratic regulation is very real. If we somehow choose to give government the dominant role in this coming partnership, will we create excessive burdens of regulation and control that destroy the sensitive market system we have evolved over the years?

It is far from clear as to whether the twenty-first century will be a world of *greater* personal freedom of thought and action. It obviously depends on how well we understand the potential and actual consequences of our actions on the future. It also depends, needless to say, on our understanding of personal freedom and our willingness to fight for it and sacrifice for it.

It may be that enlightened business leaders who understand the relationship of business to society and who have a healthy respect for individual freedom and dignity will play the most critical role in helping us to pass unscathed into the new century. This is an intriguing and real possibility if business is able to see beyond its own narrow interests to the broader interests of the public at large. I know that such leaders exist in the business community and that they are even now preaching this new gospel. The question that remains to be answered is will they be listened to? For the sake of our collective future, this may be the most important question facing our society today.

Beyond this crucial question, there are some other time bombs ticking away for us. One is the rate at which we are experiencing change. Marshall McLuhan, for one, claims that we are now living about "200 years" in a single year. Futurists of every description have commented on the increasing rate of change to which all of our institutions must adapt.

The question in the face of this careening change is whether or not we can plan adequately for the strains and stresses that all of our institutions will face. History demonstrates that when a culture is put under strain its people survive by adapting to the strain and by controlling it. If they do not adapt, the culture breaks down under the stress and that particular civilization falls and fragments into subcultures or into a new culture.

Change is difficult, but it is not fatal unless it is blindly resisted.

197

Our ability to adapt, I believe, will depend on our collective capacity to look beyond our own selfish needs. I have suggested in the two preceding chapters that we must concentrate on building effective human relationships for their own sake. The cynical organization person tends to believe that that task is hopeless and that anyone who proposes it is naive or Utopian. The fact of the matter is that given the value changes we are experiencing, given the rate of change we are experiencing, given the changing aspirations of people in American society, the cynic's solution, which generally is to get tougher with people and to pursue measurable results at all costs, is the really naive solution. It offends people's sense of who they are and what they aspire to and, in the long run, will not work because it is counter to the flow of contemporary events.

Still, as a society we are conscious of a good deal of confusion in our own minds. Is it worth the risk and the pain to try to establish effective human relationships? Can managers give up their pretensions to authority over other people in favor of guiding their work and counseling them?

Are we so success-oriented and so wedded to measurable results that we cannot break the habit? Are we so fond of our little superstitions about people that we can't bear to give them up? In short, would we rather drown in our confusion and ignorance about our lives and our institutions than face the pain of changing them and adapting to new goals, new values, new priorities?

The revolution in thought, "the scientific revolution" as Carl Madden calls it, through which we are still living, is at least as significant as the Renaissance. In the minds of some observers including Margaret Mead, it may be as profound as the change some 8,000 years ago from a hunting and gathering society to an agricultural one. And perhaps to make it worse, we are the first of the generations who have lived through cataclysmic change to be aware that we are living through it. That consciousness certainly does little for our peace of mind.

Yet there are compelling reasons for optimism. We have evolved to the point where work need no longer be unremitting drudgery. For perhaps the first time in our history the developed nations have the opportunity to make work meaningful for the mass of men and women. This is very hopeful and important.

In these same developed nations the value is emerging that people are more important than systems or things. This is largely a function of the failure of materialism in satisfying our human needs. It is also the function of increased levels of education and aspiration. And it too is a hopeful sign that society will be more attuned to its role of serving and protecting the people rather than merely using them.

Corporations, as well as our other institutional organizations, will become believable in our society again when they catch up with human need. Simply put, this means they must perform. Their performance depends on all of us, but most of all it depends on institutional leadership.

Peter Drucker says it all:

> What is needed . . . is management performance
> . . . in making work productive and the worker
> achieving, and performance with respect to the quality
> of life. But above all, it has to be performance with re-
> spect to the role and function of the manager. If he is to
> remain—as he should—the manager of an autonomous
> institution, he must accept that he is a public man. He
> must accept the moral responsibility of organization, the
> responsibility of making individual strengths productive
> and achieving.[8]

When managers understand and act on this truth, our communication problems inside and outside organizations will largely resolve themselves. If managers choose to reject this truth, our communication problems can only worsen, and will lead ultimately to even greater alienation of people from organizations and of business from society.

In the years ahead, a given corporation will be believable to the extent that it can demonstrate to its own people and to the public at large that it is conscious of more than its own narrow needs. In the face of changing public needs and aspirations, anything less than this will only worsen today's appalling credibility problems.

References

CHAPTER I
1. Peter F. Drucker, *Management: Tasks, Responsibilities, Practices* (New York: Harper & Row, 1974), pp. 490–493.
2. Drucker, p. 493.
3. Robert F. Pearse, *Manager to Manager: What Managers Think of Management Development* (New York: AMA Survey Report, 1974), pp. 49–50.

CHAPTER II
1. Interview with Harry Levinson, "Management: The Carter Phenomenon Comes to Corporations," *The New York Times,* July 16, 1976, p. 5-D.
2. M. Scott Myers, "Conditions for Manager Motivation." *New Insights for Executive Achievement* (a compilation of *Harvard Business Review* articles, 1966), pp. 11–24.

3. Daniel Bell, *The Coming of Post-Industrial Society* (New York: Basic Books, 1973), pp. 269–274.
4. Bell, pp. 287–289.

CHAPTER III
1. Warren Bennis, "Leadership: A Beleaguered Species?" *Organizational Dynamics,* Vol. 5, No. 1, 1976, pp. 3–16.
2. "Conversation with Daniel Bell," pp. 34–49.
3. John K. Galbraith, *Economics and the Public Purpose* (Boston: Houghton Mifflin, 1973), pp. 274–285.
4. Daniel Bell, *The Coming of Post-Industrial Society* (New York: Basic Books, 1973), pp. 269–298.
5. Peter F. Drucker, *Management: Tasks, Responsibilities, Practices* (New York: Harper & Row, 1974), pp. 809–811.
6. Kingman Brewster, in the annual Churchill Lecture to the English Speaking Union of the Commonwealth, London, England, November 1975.

CHAPTER IV
1. John Bailey, executive director of the International Association of Business Communicators, quoted in *The Ragan Report,* Lawrence Ragan Communications, Inc., Chicago, Ill., July 12, 1976.
2. Study by Cal Downs and Michael Hazen, reported in "Communication Satisfaction," *The Ragan Report,* Lawrence Ragan Communications, Inc., Chicago, Ill., July 5, 1976.
3. Stanley Peterfreund, *The Role of Communication in Motivation* (Englewood Cliffs, N.J.: Stanley Peterfreund Associates, 1970).
4. George de Mare in an address to the New York University–Public Relations Society of America Seminar on Employee Communication, New York City, July 1976.

CHAPTER V

1. Peter Berger, *Invitation to Sociology* (Garden City, N.Y.: Doubleday, 1963), pp. 66–92.
2. Berger, pp. 121–150.
3. Berger, pp. 149–150.
4. Robert Townsend, *Up the Organization* (New York: Knopf, 1970), p. 10.

CHAPTER VI

1. Thomas A. Murphy of General Motors in an address to the Associated Industries Annual Meeting, Lake Placid, New York, September 1976.
2. Interview with A. B. Trowbridge, "Why Business Has a Black Eye," *U.S. News and World Report*, July 14, 1975, pp. 27–30.
3. Carl H. Madden, "2008," *Across the Board* (The Conference Board Magazine), Vol. 12, No. 10, 1976, pp. 15–19.

CHAPTER VII

1. Erich Fromm, *The Sane Society* (New York: Holt, Rinehart, 1955), pp. 177–184.
2. "Employee Communications Survey 1975," a survey conducted by *The Corporate Communications Report*, January 1976, pp. 3–4.
3. "Employee Relations: Who Holds the Trump Card?" *Industry Week*, October 18, 1976, pp. 58–62.
4. Ian H. Wilson, *Corporate Environments of the Future: Planning for Major Change, Special Study No. 61* (New York: The Presidents Association of the American Management Associations, 1976), p. 9.
5. Wilson, p. 43.
6. Wilson, pp. 43–45.

CHAPTER VIII

1. Richard Cornuelle, *De-Managing America* (New York: Random House, 1975), p. 35.
2. Geoffrey Barraclough, *Management in a Changing Economy* (New York: AMA Survey Report, 1976), p. 13.
3. Cornuelle, pp. 45–46.
4. Cornuelle, pp. 82–83.
5. Barraclough, p. 13.
6. Barraclough, p. 29.
7. Barraclough, p. 42.
8. Peter F. Drucker, *Management: Tasks, Responsibilities, Practices* (New York: Harper & Row, 1974), p. 811.

Index